REVELATIONS

THE ART OF MAX BERTOLINI

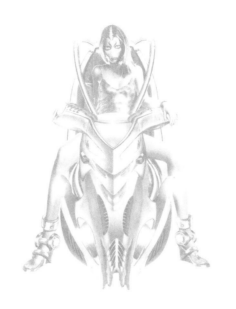

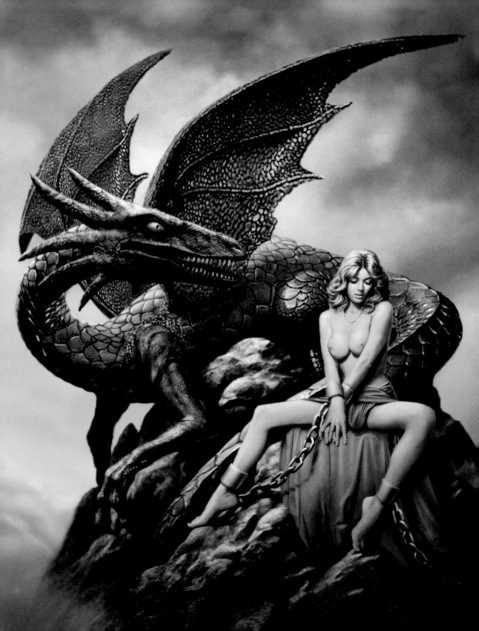

REVELATIONS

THE ART OF MAX BERTOLINI

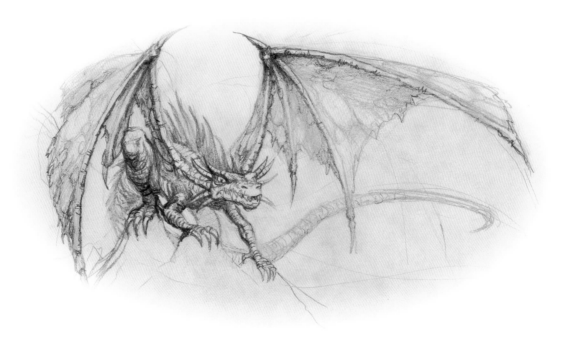

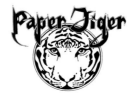

Paper Tiger

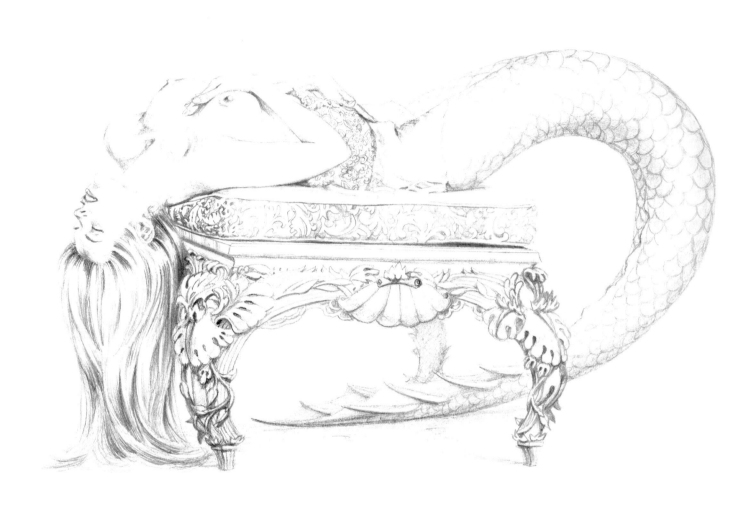

First published in Great Britain in 2005 by
Paper Tiger
The Chrysalis Building
Bramley Road
London W10 6SP

An imprint of **Chrysalis** Books Group plc

Distributed in the United States and Canada
by Sterling Publishing Co.
378 Park Avenue South, New York
NY 10016, USA

1 2 3 4 5 6 7 8 9

British Library Cataloguing-in-Publication
Data:
A catalogue record of this book is available
from the British Library.

ISBN 1 84340 225 4

Commissioning Editor: Chris Stone
Project Editor: Nicola Hodgson
Designed by: Philip Clucas MSIAD

Reproduction by: Classicscan, Singapore
Printed and bound by: Kyodo, Singapore

CONTENTS

INTRODUCTION *page 6*

CHAPTER 1
INSPIRATION *page 16*

CHAPTER 2
TECHNIQUES *page 26*

CHAPTER 3
CREATION *page 46*

CHAPTER 4
FANTASY OR SCIENCE FICTION? *page 76*

CHAPTER 5
ART AND THE MARKET *page 90*

CHAPTER 6
PIN-UPS AND EROTIC ART *page 98*

ART INDEX *page 126*

ACKNOWLEDGEMENTS *page 128*

INTRODUCTION

When I was a child I wanted be an astronaut. Most children want this at one time or another, but the lure of space was particularly strong in me, a feeling driven by pure desire. I was fascinated by the sense of infinite mystery that the cosmos transmits, and I wanted to explore it. I still remember with a feeling of great nostalgia the silver spacesuit my parents bought me for a carnival. *First Contact*, the illustration in which two astronauts stare at the alien heads carved on a rock outcrop, conveys perfectly what I am trying to say. In the 1970s, when I was still very young, it really did seem that human colonization of the cosmos was imminent: lunar missions came and went, and television viewers were treated to numerous excellent sci-fi dramas, such as *UFO* and *Space 1999*. My father had a vast collection of science-fiction novels, which I used to devour with gusto, always finishing, however, with the wish that I could, in some way, re-create in reality those worlds that I had been reading about. I also used to read lots of American comics, and the colourful heroes and their superpowers used to leave me breathless. I felt an instinctive attraction to the human body in motion: I loved the energy of those muscular bodies and the grace of the women. However, it wasn't this that influenced me the most: I simply had a strong natural inclination to let my

FIRST CONTACT

Right: Digital, cover for *Fantasy & Science-Fiction Magazine*, *Galaxies* and AST Publisher

I wanted to give an impression of majestic antiquity and the surprise that astronauts might feel on discovering such a monument on a faraway planet, a symbol of an ancient but now vanished alien civilization.

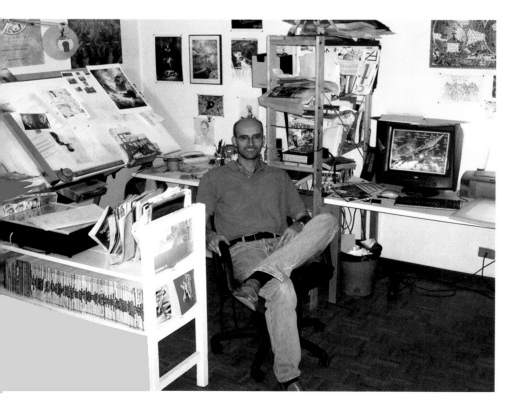

Left: The Studio
On the left is the universal drafting device, full of the pages of all the new projects I'm working on. On the right is my computer, while the other walls are lined with bookshelves. Keeping all my reference material and all my drawing tools together in a single dedicated place helps me create the best environment for developing new ideas.

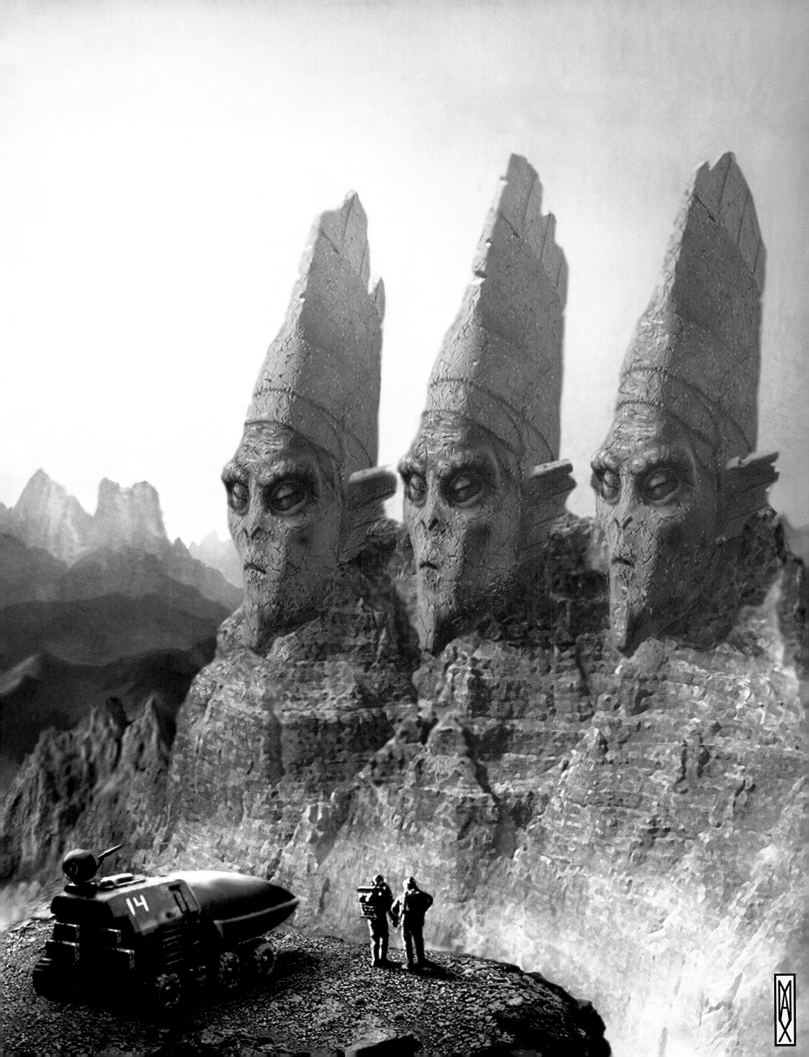

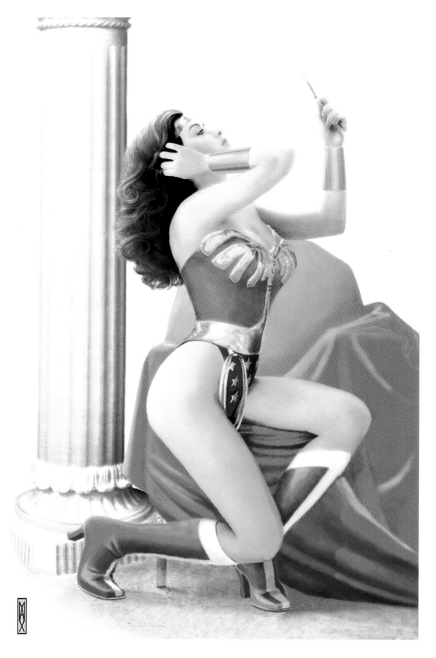

WONDER WOMAN

Left: Digital, private work, © DC Comics

I wanted to show a powerful superheroine behaving like a normal woman. I like colours that are inspired by the pin-up girls of the 1940s and 1950s.

Below: Pencil on board, 8.5 x 11.5 inches, Private work, © DC Comics

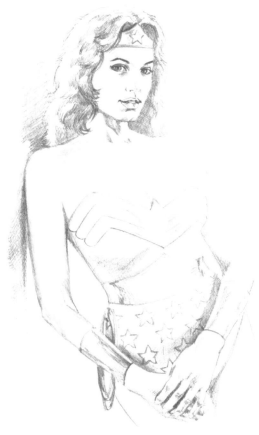

BATMAN

Right: Digital, private work, © DC Comics

It's hard for me, as a fan of superheroes, to avoid the fascination of the dark night. Here is my homage to the most complex and tragically appealing crime fighter in the superheroes pantheon. I tried to give the costume and the atmosphere the dark feeling of the vision that creator Bob Kane originally had in mind in 1939.

imagination run wild, and I soaked up everything and anything that could feed it. Although I didn't know it at the time, I would eventually return to and reproduce in new forms everything that I had seen and read.

I had a certain predisposition towards drawing – I was irresistibly attracted by the huge white spaces on pieces of paper and eagerly filled them with intergalactic battles and astronauts. The 1970s were also the boom years of the great British sci-fi illustrators, and I was fascinated by the way they so realistically used to re-create my dreams before my eyes. I had a burning desire to be able to do this too. I had to. And I succeeded, but not immediately. Having attained my middle-school diploma, I thought about going to art school, but the difficulty I believed I would later have in finding a job combined with the ease with which I coped with academic work in general led me to choose an awful science-oriented high school. However, I can say, with hindsight, that the choice I made,

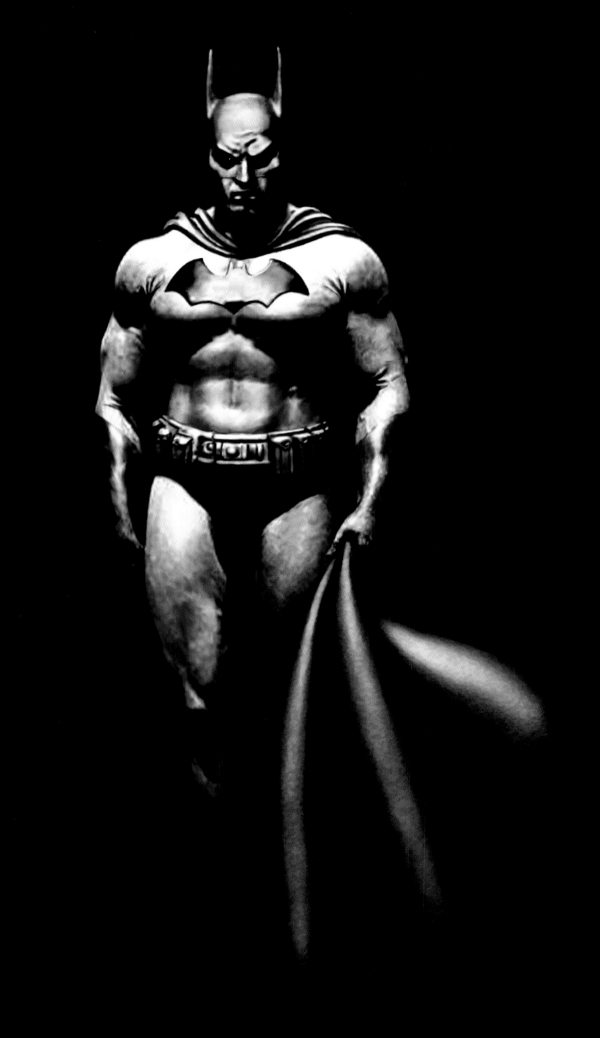

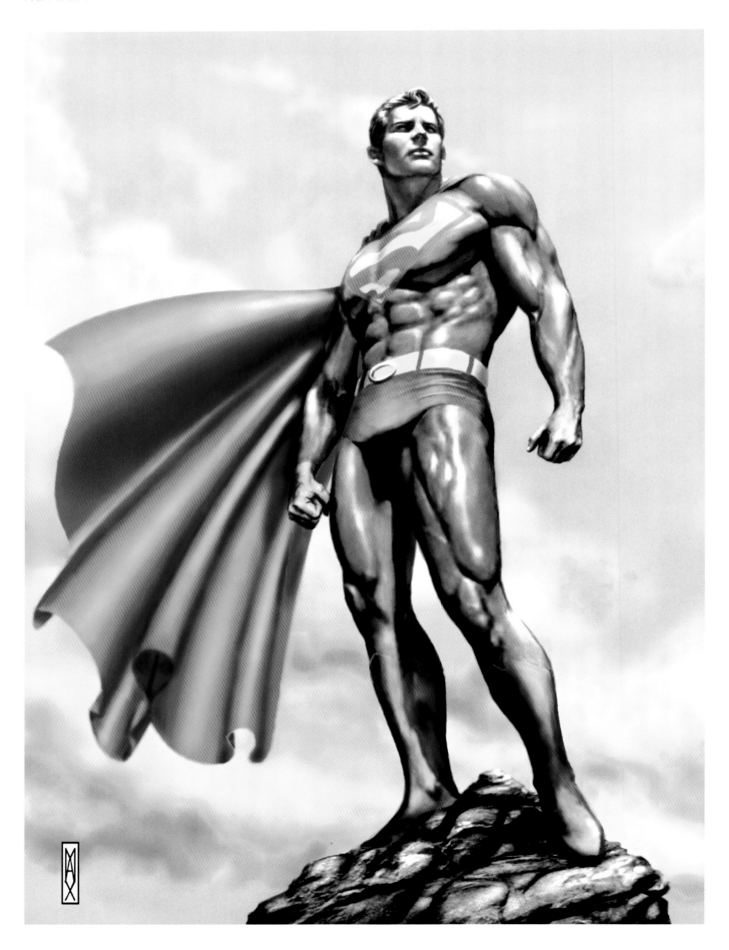

SUPERMAN

Left: Digital, cover for *Comic US Summer Special*,
© DC Comics

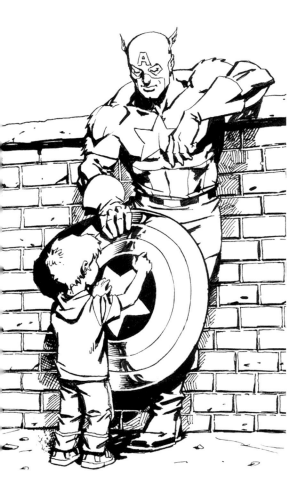

CAPTAIN AMERICA

Above: Ink on paper, 8.5 x 11.5 inches, inside
illustration for *Homage to Jack Kirby*, Comicus,
© Marvel Comics

In this drawing the fascination this child feels
for the superhero's weapon is the same I felt
as a young reader when I used to turn over
the pages of those amazing comic books.

PAGE FROM NATHAN NEVER

Right: Ink on paper, 8.5 x 11.5 inches,
© Sergio Bonelli Editore

In this page the graveyard of the planes is a
homage to J.K. Potter's illustration *Memories of
the Space Age II*.

although somewhat removed from my aspirations, gave me a rational
approach to work and helped me to avoid eccentricity and inconsistency
that are sometimes found in artists who went to art school.

After high school I went to university to study Modern Languages and
Literature, but the desire still burned within me, and I finally realized that
I had made too many mistakes in my life. Now I had to try and do what I
really wanted. I had never stopped drawing, but it was something I did as
a hobby, without any tuition, just as I always had done. Thinking about it
now, I believe this really showed my inclination for drawing. Even though
I did it without any guidance, I had no problems in understanding the
fundamental principles of art: anatomy, perspective, the use of shade and
composition. Everything came to me quite easily. I studied magazines to
see how my future colleagues worked, and if I had any doubts I would read
books on design, quickly absorbing the information on offer. I started
doing a few short cartoons for a Milanese fanzine, I went around a few
publishing houses, and then I did some trial storyboards for *Nathan Never*,
a highly successful science-fiction comic book that had just appeared on
the newsstands. The series editor was struck by how my drawings were

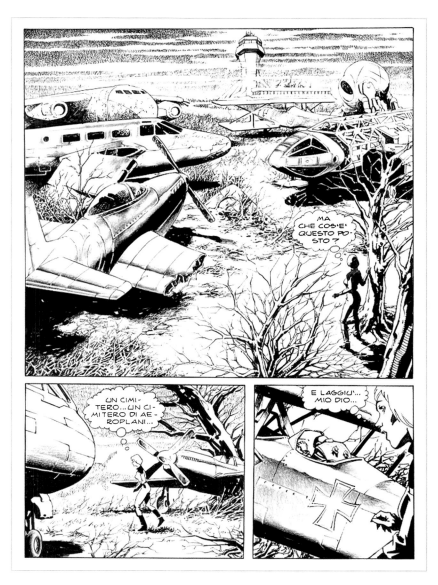

PAGE FROM
NATHAN NEVER No. 143

Right: Ink on paper, 8.5 x 11.5 inches,
© Sergio Bonelli Editore

PANEL FROM
NATHAN NEVER No. 103

Below: Ink on paper, © Sergio Bonelli Editore

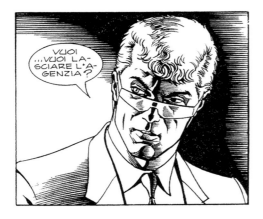

PAGE FROM
NATHAN NEVER No.103

Opposite page: Ink on paper, 8.5 x 11.5 inches,
© Sergio Bonelli Editore

PANEL FROM
AGENZIA ALFA No. 6

Below: Ink on paper, © Sergio Bonelli Editore

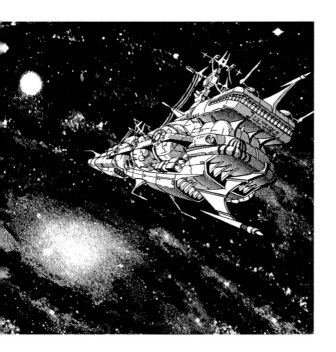

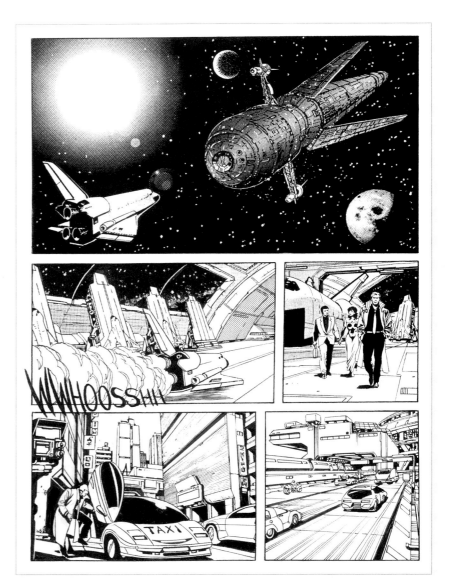

improving frame-by-frame, and within a couple of months I was given my first story.

For a few years I dedicated myself almost entirely to black-and-white drawings, but I eventually began to feel that this was no longer enough: I needed to express my emotions in another way. I therefore started using colours – first oil paints and then virtual colours using a computer monitor. I feel more comfortable doing illustrations because instead of working on an infinite series of panels, I can instead concentrate on a single image, making it as effective as possible. I feel that my work is somehow more complete in this way.

I received the first cheque for my *Nathan Never* drawings in 1993 and from that moment I have made a living solely from my art. The colonization of space has taken slightly longer than I hoped, but I'm still here waiting, ready with my silver spacesuit.

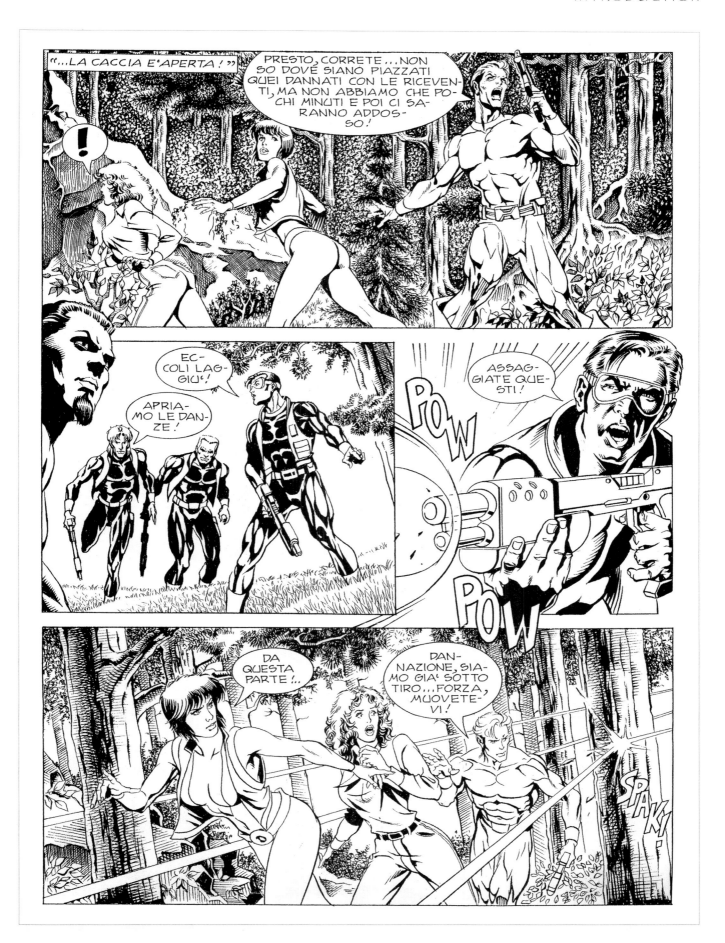

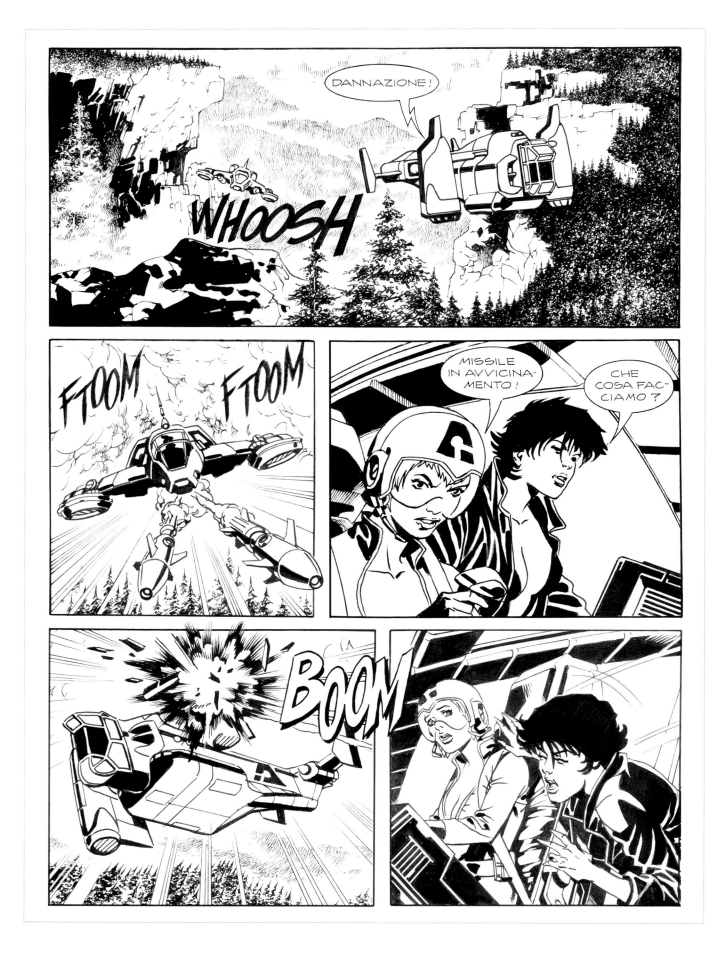

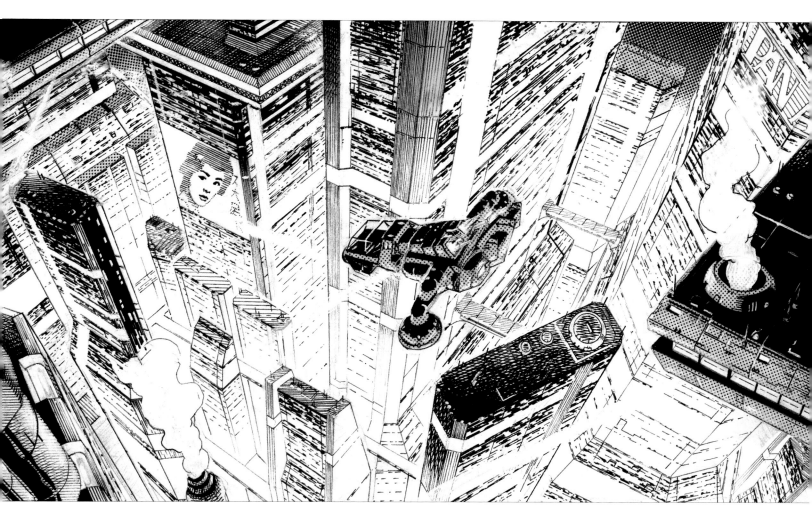

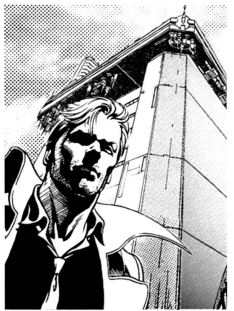

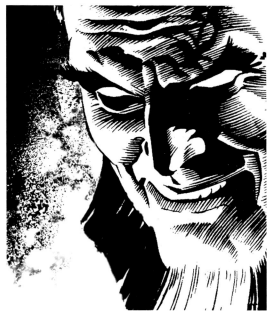

PANEL FROM

NATHAN NEVER

Above: Ink on paper, 8 x 4 inches,
© Sergio Bonelli Editore

Originally a simple panel I drew for
the comic book *Nathan Never*, this
was afterwards the starting
point for the painting *Star City*
(see page 93).

PANELS FROM

NATHAN NEVER

Left and far left: Ink on paper,
© Sergio Bonelli Editore

PAGE FROM

NATHAN NEVER No. 156

Left: Ink on paper, 8.5 x 11.5 inches, © Sergio Bonelli Editore

INSPIRATION

I t is difficult to talk about something – such as the imagination – whose roots are buried deep in the subconscious. On the whole, I would say that there are two major sources of inspiration for my work: the visual and the emotional. The visual aspect is the easier to comprehend and is a result of the vast array of images I have come across and mentally filed away over the years: films, the paintings of classic artists I love, the work of colleagues, advertising, cartoons, photography and so on. Over time, this mass of images has settled in my subconscious, and I instinctively extract and rework them when I have to create something new. When I look closely at one of my finished illustrations, I often end up saying, 'This is reminiscent of the colours in that Vermeer painting,' or 'This one is Caravaggio-esque in the dramatic power of the subject'. Sometimes, I can't quite trace the source of my visual inspiration, but I do believe that it is difficult to create something genuinely original not only in fantasy illustration, but more generally in all kinds of art, and so a certain humility, acquired after years in this profession, prevents me from believing that I have created something completely new. Let's just say that I am always satisfied when I think I have produced something that is aesthetically pleasing and sufficiently original in itself.

When it comes to settings, I am often inspired by the mountain landscapes I have seen. The background of some of my illustrations was inspired by the ruggedness of the Dolomites in northern Italy, which I particularly love for their imposing stature and the sense of history they invoke in me. When I am surrounded by their silence, the thoughts that run through my head form into images, and I feel closer to the limitless space of the universe, far from the grey of Milan, where I live.

Emotional inspiration is a different matter entirely and is much more elusive and more difficult to explain. It is the transposition onto paper of a feeling, an emotion, a thought that I am trying to transmit to the viewer. Sometimes it is a piece of music, more often it is a story. It is without doubt more difficult to translate one's emotions onto a piece of paper than to reproduce a simple image born out of fantasy, but when this operation is successful, the results are nearly always preferable. Almost all of my best illustrations belong to the former category and are enjoyed by everyone, regardless of the subject, because they have a universal dimension. When sentiment is present in a drawing, it speaks to everybody in the same language and goes straight to the heart of everyone who looks at it. When my work is driven by a particular emotion, I have more energy and enthusiasm, and this is inevitably apparent in the final result. In the majority of cases, however, visual and emotional inspiration are mixed together in different proportions in the creation of a new piece of work.

DRAGON RIDE

Left: Digital, cover for AST Publisher

When I imagined the scene I had to think up a way to show fairly well the girl riding the dragon and the dragon itself, which had to be quite bigger. So I decided to represent the foreground of the head of the dragon, with the girl at the top, and its wide wing in the background, leaving to imagination how big the beast could be.

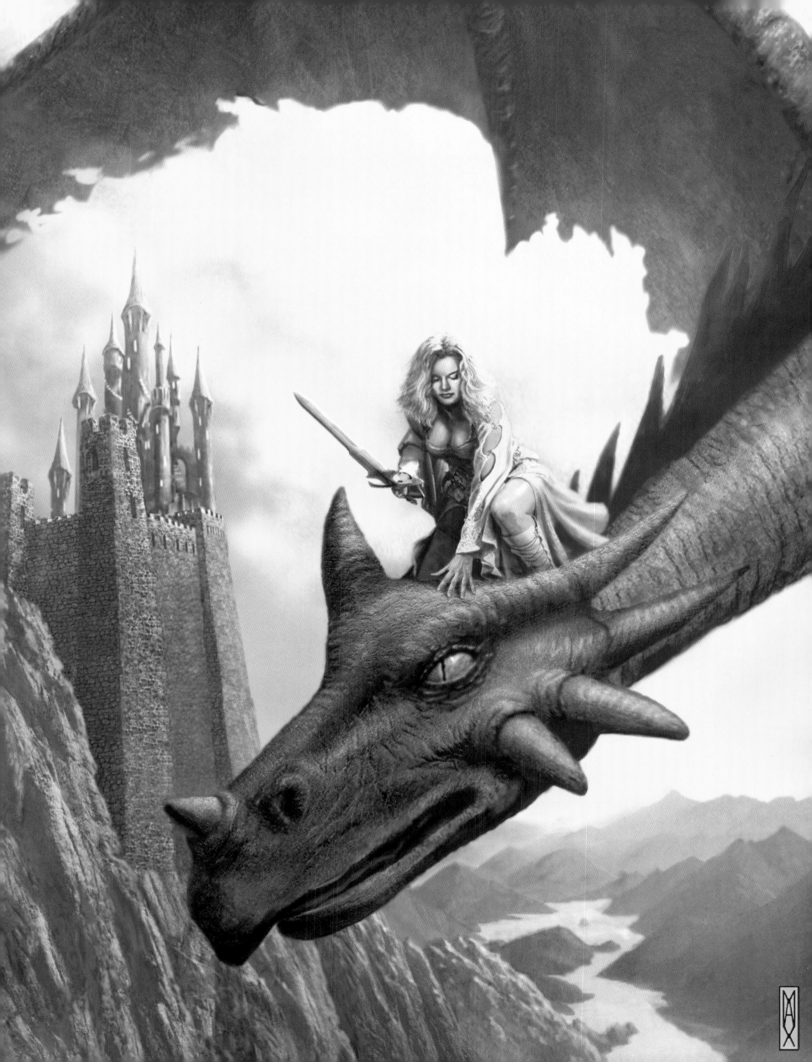

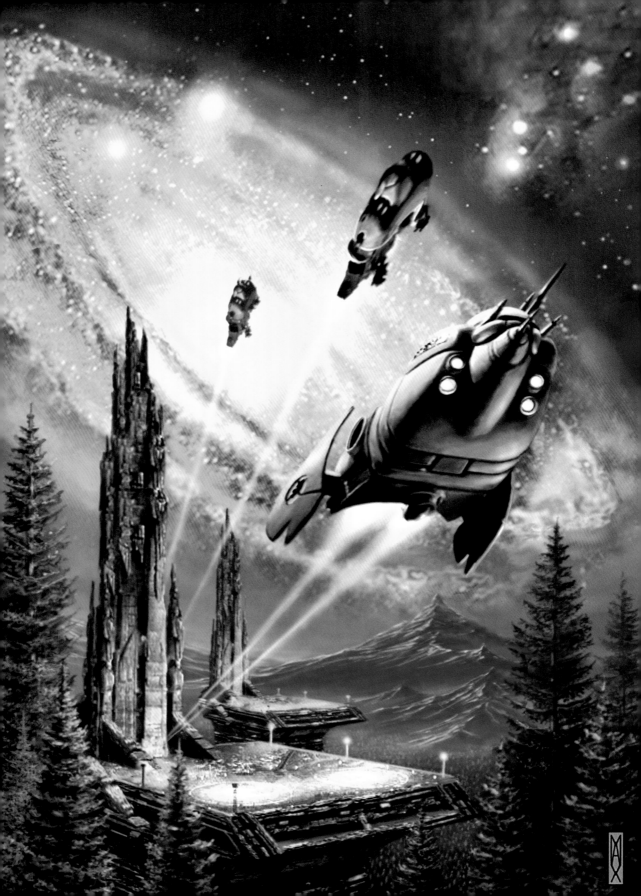

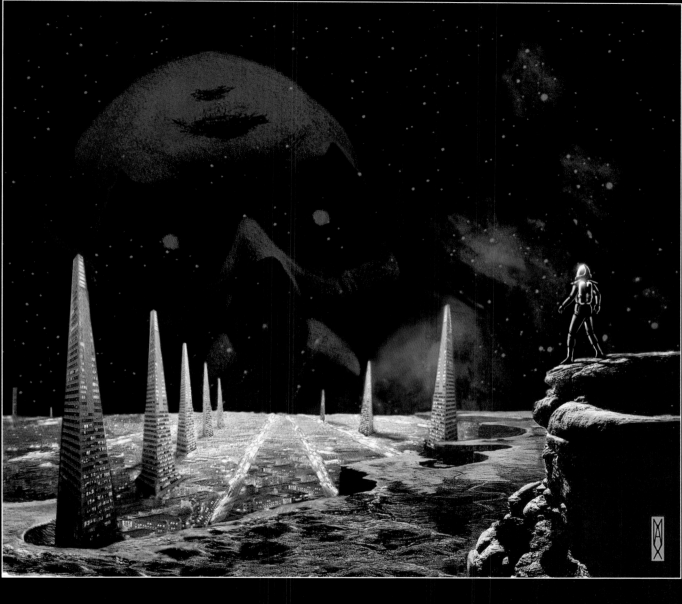

THE GOD IN THE SKY

Above: Digital, private work

I tried to create a strong evocative mood with this illustration. A solitary man on top of a rock faces an omnipotent alien presence in the sky. The result of the battle is not important: what's important is the courage that is demonstrated.

STAR CORE

Left: Digital, private work

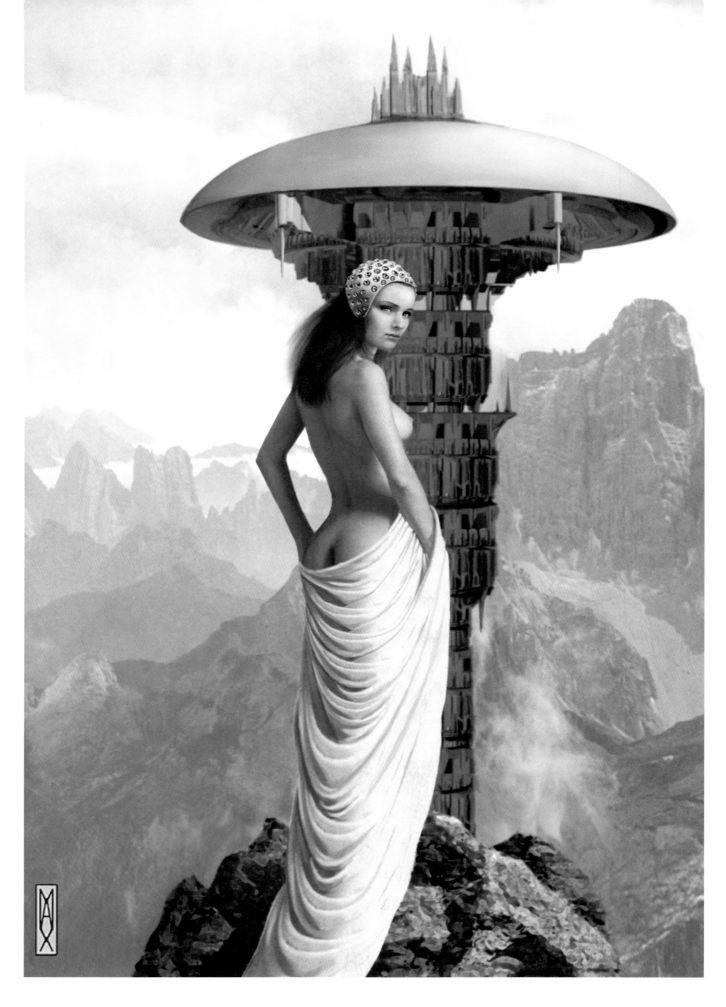

20

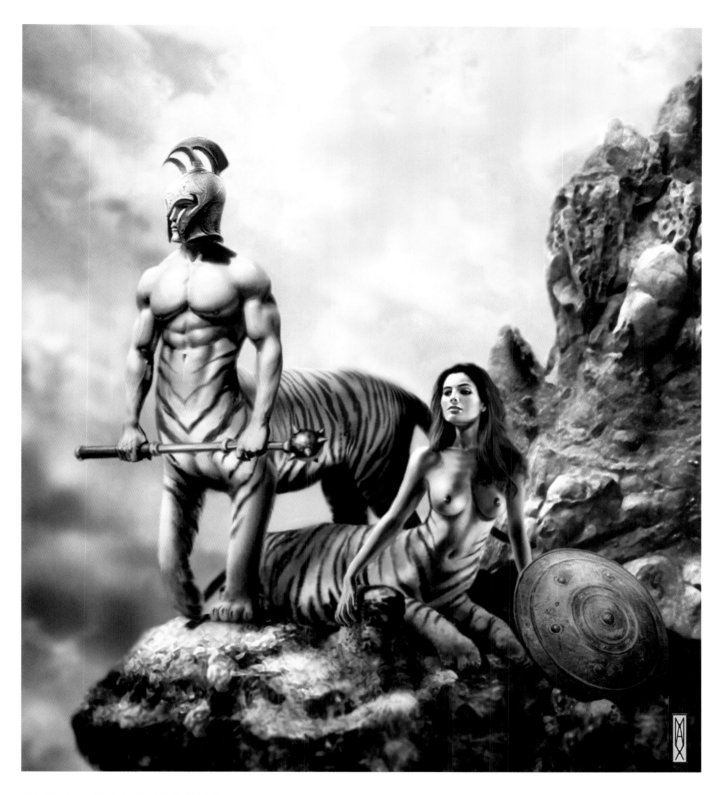

SHE DWELLS AMONG THE CLOUDS

Left: Digital, cover for Eura Editoriale

The Snow Queen. I tried to balance the livid colours of the sky with her skin tone, while maintaining the contrast of the colours with the background. I can't help but shiver with cold whenever I look at her!

THE TIGER WARRIORS

Above: Digital, unpublished

The realm of fantasy is rife with creatures both monstrous and awe-inspiring. I used tigers instead of horses, trying a new take on an old idea. I worked hard to merge the feline and human anatomies, and created a wild background appropriate for my tiger warriors.

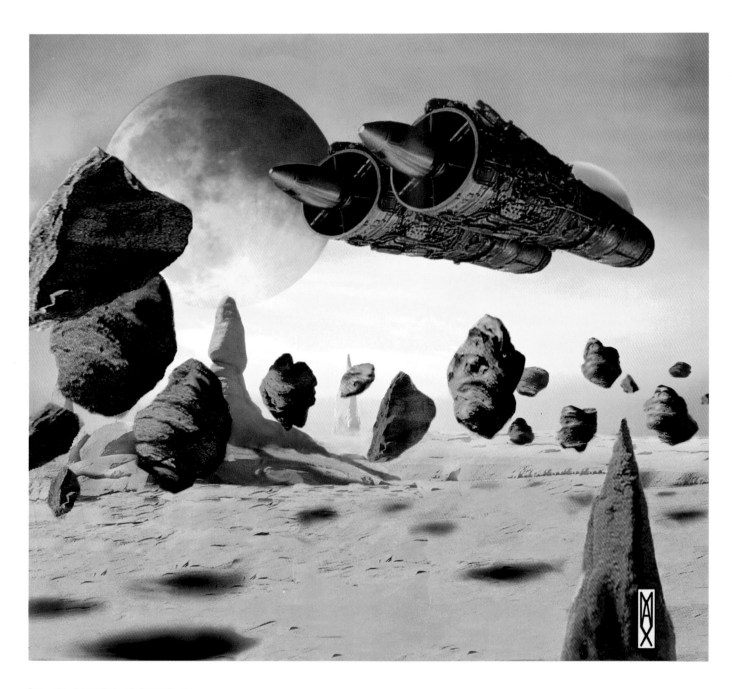

THE EXPLORERS

Above: Digital, private work

A faraway time and place. An alien ship flies
slowly over an uninhabited planet. There is
silence and a mysterious sensation of calm.

STORM

Right: Digital, private work

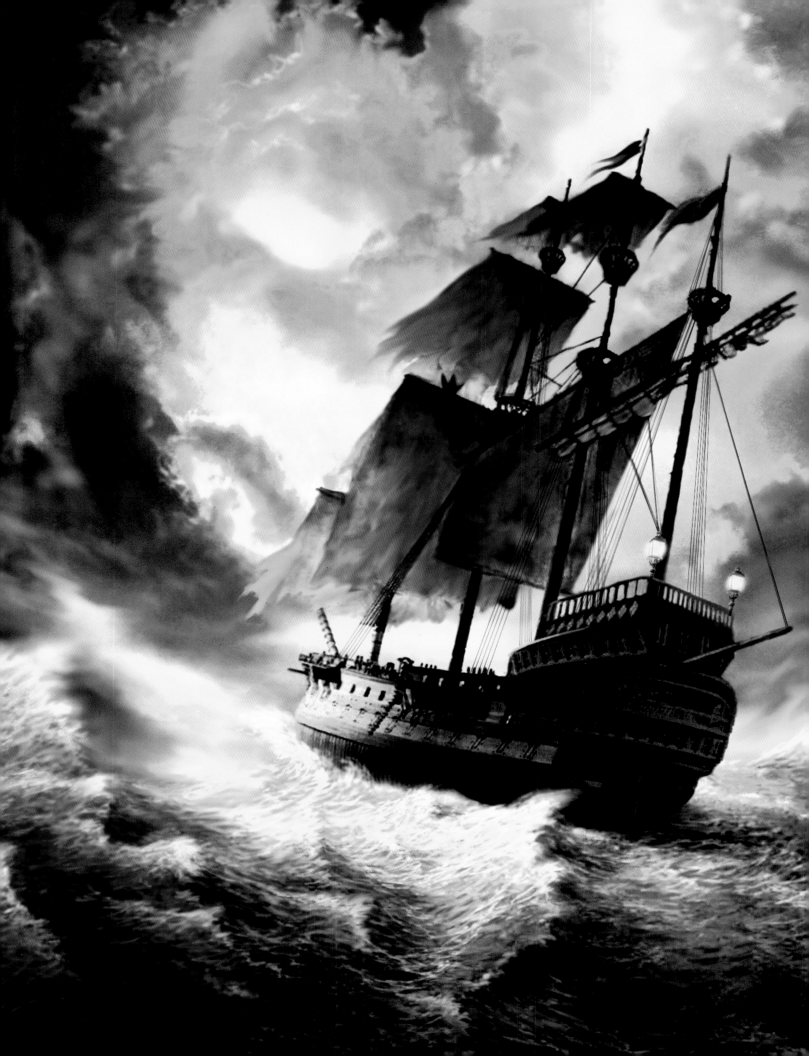

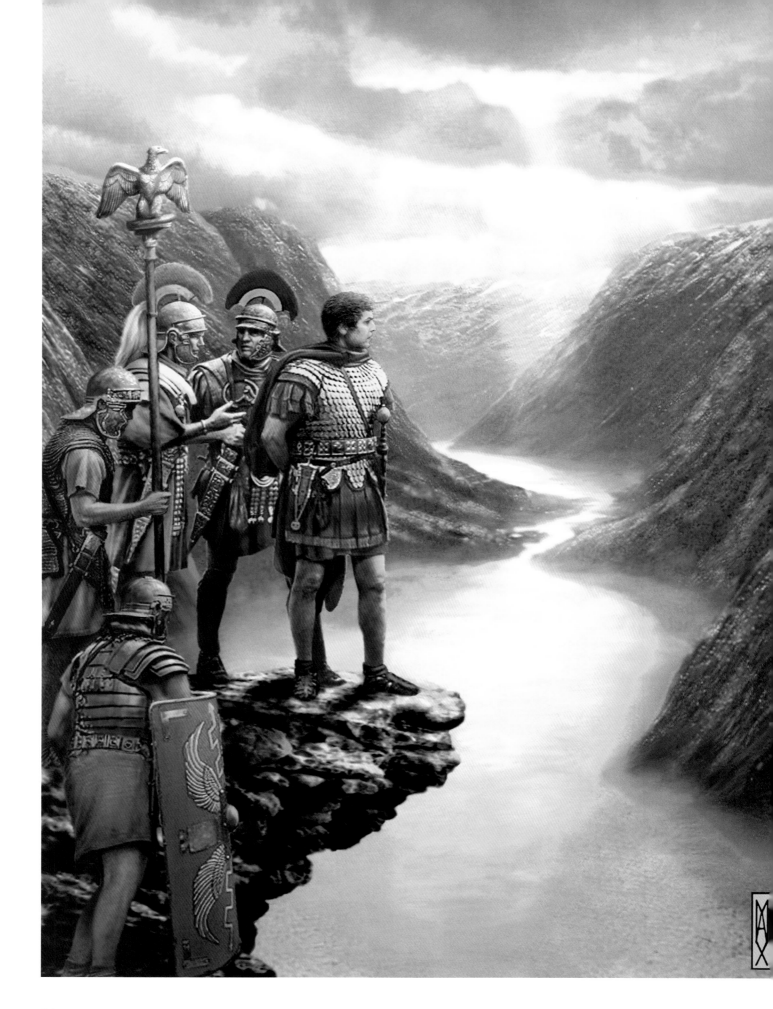

LAST ROMAN CONQUER

Left: Digital, private work

This is one of my favourites. I imagined a Roman patrol arriving at the extreme limit of the known world. The vision of the wild landscape fills the officers with dismay, but the commander is wondering on whether to continue and step forward into the unknown.

I find it hard to combine sentiment and technique when I work on a commissioned piece because the idea that I have been given may not be one that I particularly like. It is easy to spot when an artist has worked using just technique, without passion. The result will be cold, even if it satisfies the client, who often won't realize that what he has in front of him is simply a decent exercise in style. If, on the other hand, it is thought that a drawing has been done with some degree of passion, it will sell more easily because it touches a larger proportion of the public: sentiment and market success often go hand-in-hand. A few of my more dreamlike illustrations have been bought numerous times by different editors precisely because they convey a feeling rather than just narrating an action.

However, both the emotional aspect and the imaginative capacity must be constantly nourished: they are like a tree that bears fruit only if it is correctly cultivated. Many of my ideas come from far away, from childhood images, but I continually watch films and television programmes and study the work of better artists than me in the hope that I can absorb ideas and then later reproduce them in new ways. Sometimes life's experiences act as my inspiration. I have seen how dangerous it is for artists to shut themselves away in their studios, limiting their contact with the outside world. They run the risk of continuously producing the same things, ever-paler imitations of the same idea. When I have a good idea I don't forget it, and sooner or later I manage to use it. But how do you recognize a good idea? For me it is the emotional impact it has on me and the pressing desire I have to realize it. I am not bothered if somebody else has already had the idea (which is likely given that original ideas are so rare), but I rely on the fact that my enthusiasm will enable me to rework it in a new and fascinating manner, and add something of myself to the final result. It is not as important to come up with new ideas, but rather to add a personal touch to things that we have already seen, because we each have a unique personality that comes through in everything we create. If we are truly successful in this operation, we will have a good chance of making our work unique and distinctive, even among that of the many professional artists out there. When an illustrator has reached a fair level of technical accomplishment (and, sooner or later, with a bit of application, this is a landmark that will be reached) this is the only way of doing memorable work .

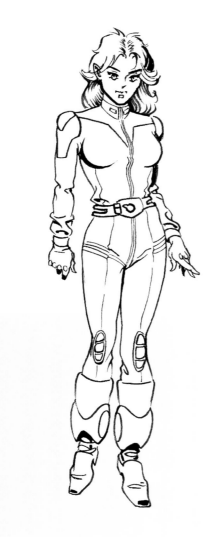

SARA

Left: Ink on paper,
2 x 4 inches,
private work.

A simple sketch in manga style, done just for fun.

TECHNIQUES

My journey from paper to the screen came about after a period of reflection about the technique I was using in my work. I had already begun to do illustrations, but using traditional techniques - oil or watercolour pencils. The results were quite good, but I felt that, for the way in which I conceived the creation of an illustration, these techniques were not the most suitable. I needed a method that would enable me to make any kind of change at any moment during my work, and this was certainly not a possibility using traditional techniques. I already knew a little bit about computers, but I also feared them because I didn't want to entrust the construction of one of my images to a machine that could break down at any moment. I also worried about the complexity of the processes involved, and I didn't want to have to become an IT expert to do my drawings. I wanted to take this step, but at the same time it scared me. The situation was finally resolved by my wife. One Saturday morning she dragged me to the Apple shop where, in one fell swoop, I bought the entire system I work with today. When they delivered the equipment I found myself with a worrying pile of cables, monitors, keyboards and peripherals, which stared at me from the other side of the room like some kind of alien being. I was fascinated by the possibilities that it promised and cautiously made my way towards it. I didn't yet know exactly how it worked and I was scared to touch it in case I broke anything. So, each night, I set up a different piece and attempted to understand how it was used. Even then I did everything on my own, my passion and curiosity instilling me with an unwavering desire. My only companion was the Macintosh manual. By day I was Dr Jekyll, working in the traditional way with brushes and tubes of colour, but come the evening I was Mr Hyde, exploring the world of virtual design. Every night I discovered something new, and this mysterious presence in my house seemed less and less terrifying and ever more friendly, slowly revealing all its secrets to me.

For a time I had shared my studio with a website designer, and I distinctly remember saying to him: 'I don't want anything to do with computers because they are too unreliable. The pencil, on the other hand, will never betray me!' I'll never forget the look on his face when, some time later, he saw the system I had bought and the things I could do with it.

It was a gamble that I can now say paid off, and it taught me not to fear new things and always to look slightly beyond my own back garden. Now I'm able to produce a good illustration in under five days whereas, when I was working with oil, it took me at least twenty. This is a great advantage, not just in terms of time, but also from an emotional point of view. Taking too long over a piece of work used to be frustrating because I'd often come up with a new idea in the meantime that I couldn't wait to get started on.

SILVER SURFER

Right: Pencil on paper and digital, private work, © Marvel Comics

I imported the image, originally a drawing in coloured pencil, into Photoshop, where I added the final effects.

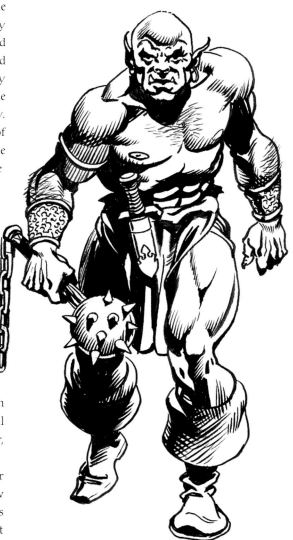

TROLL

Above: Ink on paper, 5 x 8 inches, private work.

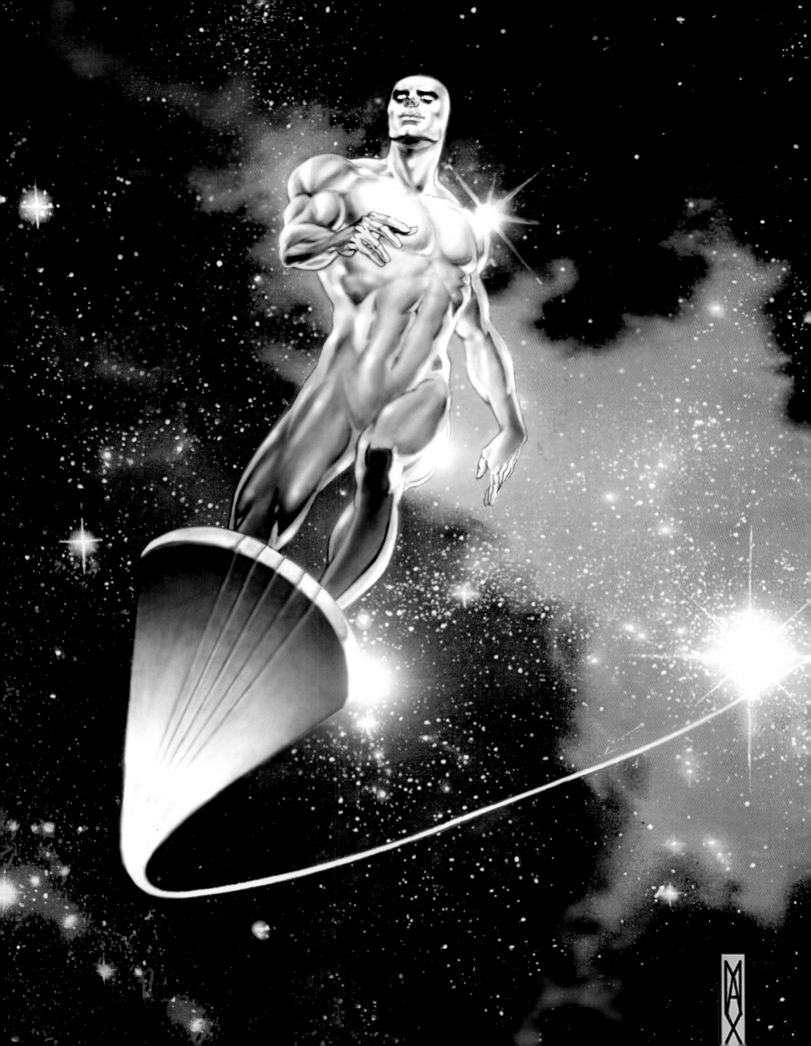

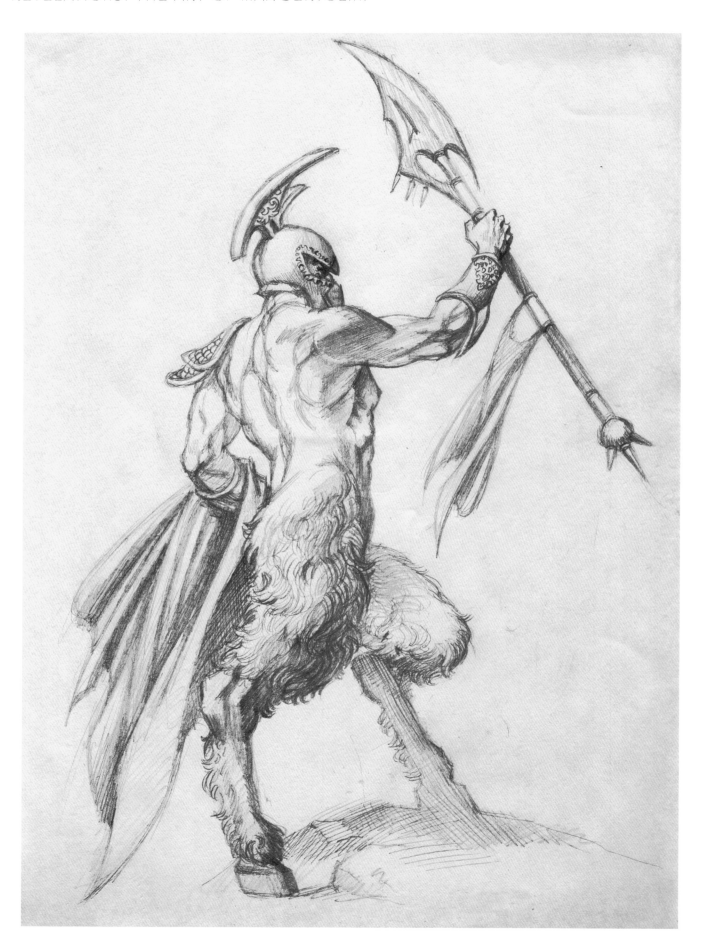

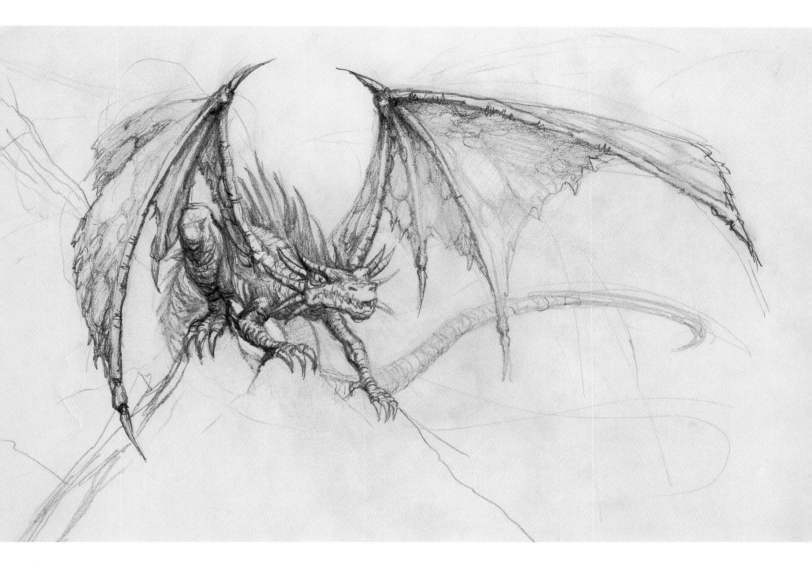

DRAGON (above)
SATYR (left)
SMILODON (right)

I love pencil drawings. They have a softness that is hard to achieve with other media. I was interested in giving a feeling of 'antiquity' to these pieces, so I used shades of red on a yellow background. My main aim was to find the right balance of chiaroscuro, so I invented the satyr's outfit and weapon only while I was drawing.

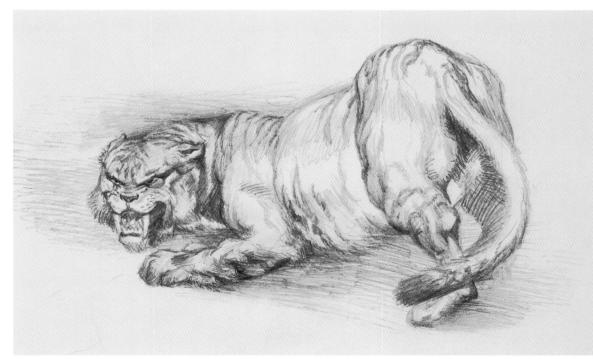

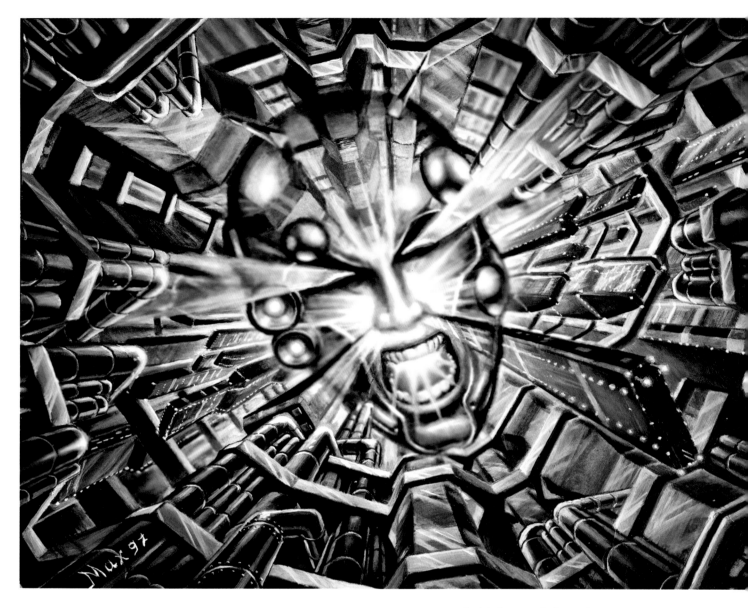

I still work by hand on black–and–white comics and I never use the computer, not even for dot tints, which I don't use very often anymore, in any case.

My approach to digital illustration is that of an artist who uses the monitor as if it were a piece of drawing paper. As mentioned in the Introduction, I am a self-taught designer, who practised traditional methods. I studied everything that could help me create my worlds on the blank page: anatomy, perspective, composition, colouring techniques and the use of black and white, the last being particularly useful for cartoons. A computer is of no practical use if you don't already know how to draw.

Having come up with a good idea, the next step is, of course, to put it into effect, and this is where things start to get a little tricky. The first step is to find a good photographic frame of reference, without which you run the risk of producing something too flat or too cartoonish. Sometimes this phase can take a whole day, but it is time well spent. Only a good, realistic area of shadowing, which is based on a photograph, can create the illusion of the three-dimensional nature of a drawing, and nowadays almost all professional

TECHNICAL CHRIME

Above: Oil on art board, 11 x 11 inches, cover for *Technical Chrime*, heavy metal CD by Node, Lucretia Records

This illustration was commissioned for the CD cover of a heavy metal band. I tried to create a sense of oppression and explosive violence. Originally an oil on art board, the image was later touched up on computer to make the shading more subtle.

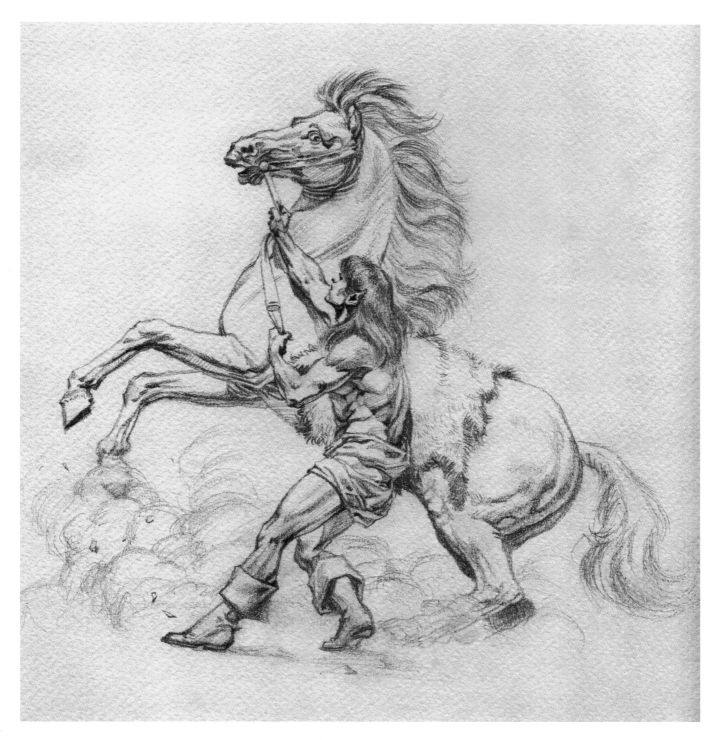

HORSE OF MARLY

Above: Pencil on paper

I drew this while I was looking at Guillaume Coustou's *Horse Tamer*, the sculpture from the château of Marly, now in the Louvre Museum, Paris.

illustrators work from photographic references, unless they happen to use 3D programs. I'm not a fan of 3D illustrations because the perfect light that these programs typically produce leaves the image cold and plastic-like, and, to the trained eye, it is immediately evident that the textures used are artificial. This is not to say, however, that a good 3D design doesn't exert a certain fascination, particularly on young people who love the hyper-realism of the images. When I have found all my reference material, which I often produce myself by taking photographs, I do a pencil drawing, which I then colour with watercolour pencils. Sometimes, depending on the amount of realism I want in the final image, I start drawing on the photograph itself after

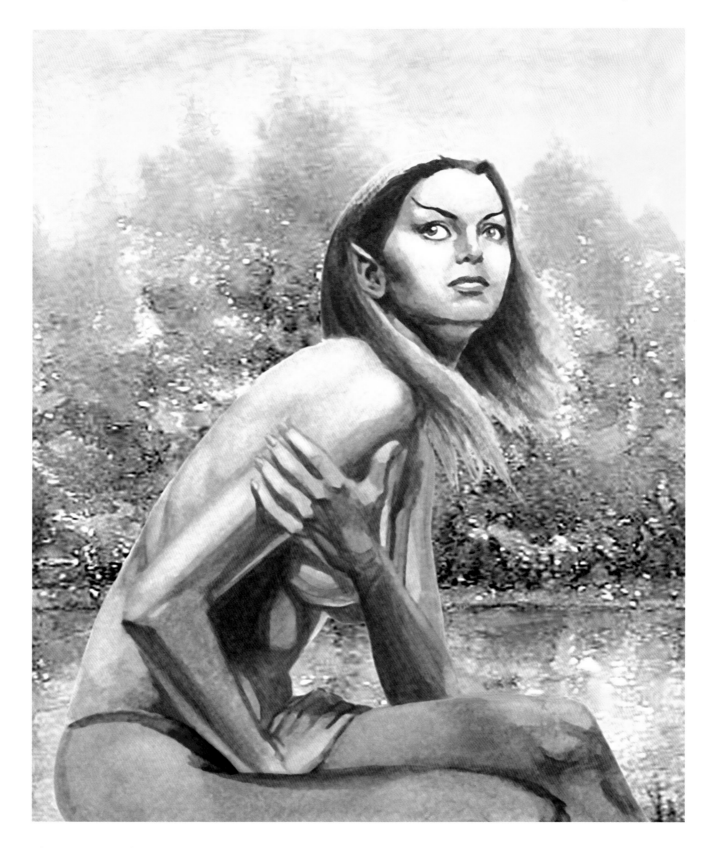

ON THE LAKE

Above: Watercolour on paper, 8.5 x 11.5 inches, private work

SILENT WATCHER

Digital, private work. Using Photoshop, I made a copy of the image and laid it on top. Then I desaturated the new layer and turned it to transparent red. This made the illustration uniform, without changing the balance of chiaroscuro.

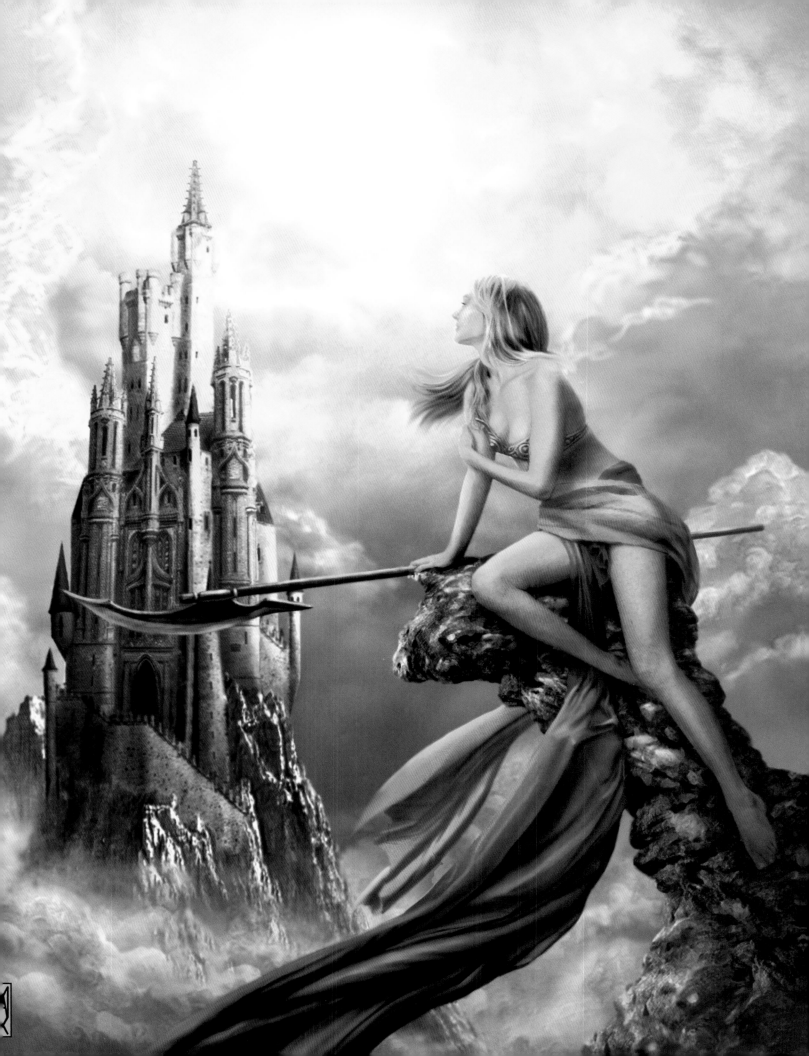

importing it onto the computer, looking at the original lights and shadows of the photo to achieve perfect realism. Before taking the photographs, I quickly make a few rough sketches of the positions that I want the models to take up, according to the illustration I have in mind. When I'm on the set I like to have complete control over the image. I study the poses of the models closely as well as the hang of the clothes because I want the photos to be similar to the prepared drawings. To be sure of the result, I take more than one photograph of the same pose from different angles. For me the models are mannequins – I position them and move them around as I see fit. If I have some degree of camaraderie with them, so much the better – everything becomes much simpler and the photos are taken more quickly. Usually, after about an hour of photography, the models begin to get into the swing of things and interpret their parts more effectively, sometimes even improvising situations for the drawings.

The photographic stage over, the illustrative work begins. But how can you have the same dexterity with a computer that brushes allow you? What is required are a good graphics tablet and an optical pen. Forget about creating decent computer designs using a mouse – at the most this will let you work on colours and light, more graphic work than can be done by hand. With an optical pen, however, you have a tool that you can use as an airbrush, a paintbrush or a pencil. And that is not all: you can calibrate both the pressure and the angle of the pen so that it adapts to your own level of skill. For an illustrator, the difference between a mouse and an optical pen is similar to that between a moped and a space shuttle. My graphics tablet is a WACOM A4 oversize, almost A3 in format. It is important to have a spacious work surface – you gain in precision without having to enlarge the details too much. When it comes to graphics programs, I use only Photoshop.

The optical pen enables me to work at my best, using all the airbrush options from the tools menu, selecting the brush size that I require as and when I need it. By increasing the size of the image, I can work with greater precision on the smallest of details without having to strain my eyes too much, as one does when working on paper.

This is the technique that I use, although it will not be appropriate for everybody. When I show my work to the students at the art school where I teach, their first questions are always: How did you do that? What techniques do you use? These are perfectly normal, and I am happy to explain exactly how I work, but when they then try to do some drawings using my methods, they are rarely satisfied with the results. It is always interesting to study the different techniques that professionals use, but it can also be misleading, because over time, every artist develops their own particular technique that responds to their requirements and characteristics and is therefore something extremely personal. What works for me may not work for others because all artists have their own individual idiosyncrasies and will search for a method that satisfies them. Some do this successfully with watercolours, some with oils, others with tempera. It is good to try working in every type of medium, but we shouldn't think that just because we are not proficient with one technique, we won't be capable of producing anything of merit. It just means that we haven't yet found the right method for us.

THE RAPTURE

Right: Oil on paper, 8.5 x 11.5 inches, private work

A hot night, a slight breeze and a huge moon in the sky … but one must never let down one's guard! I imported the image, originally an oil painting, into Photoshop, where I added the final effects: desaturation, a blurring of the background and a few corrections to the clouds. It is a homage to the heroic fantasy genre, with a romantic tinge.

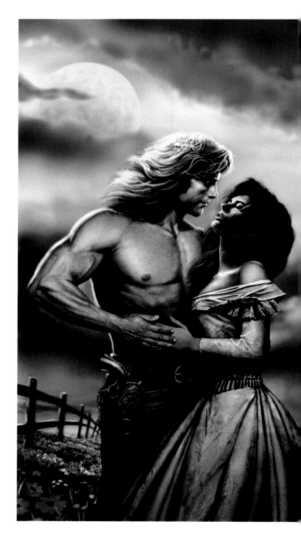

THE OUTLAW
AND THE LADY

Above: Digital, cover for *Prendimi e portami via*, *I Rosa*, Arnoldo Mondadori Editore

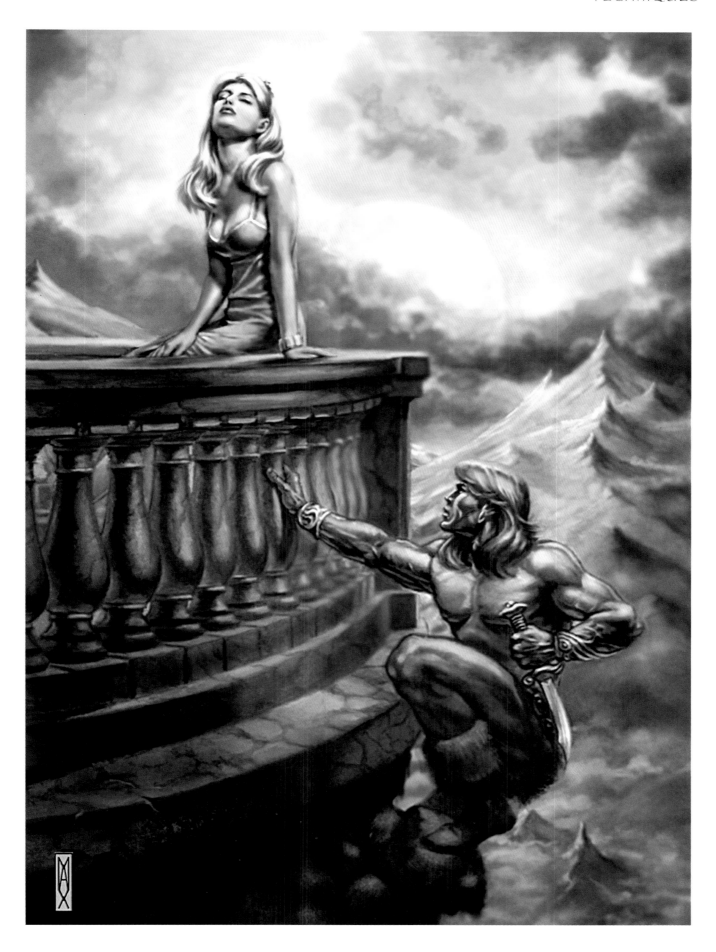

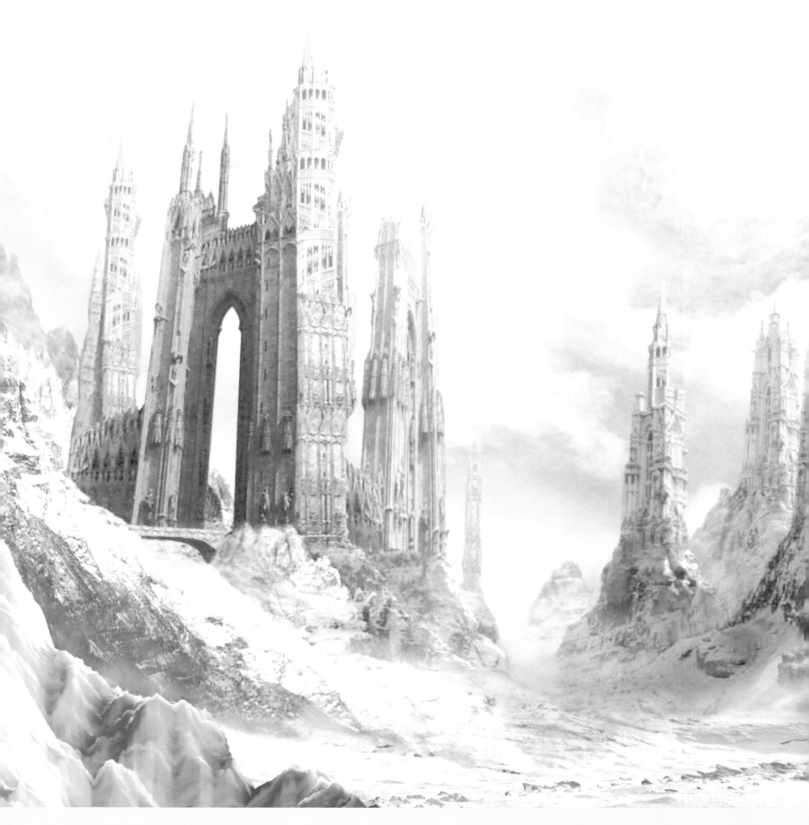

FROZEN PLANET

Above: Digital, advertisement for Diesel. This is the landscape of the cloudy planet of the Evil Emperor, whose castle rises from the snowy mountains. A giant print (about 89 x 55 inches) of this illustration was used as the background for mannequins in stores. I brought many different architectural elements together as accurately as I could.

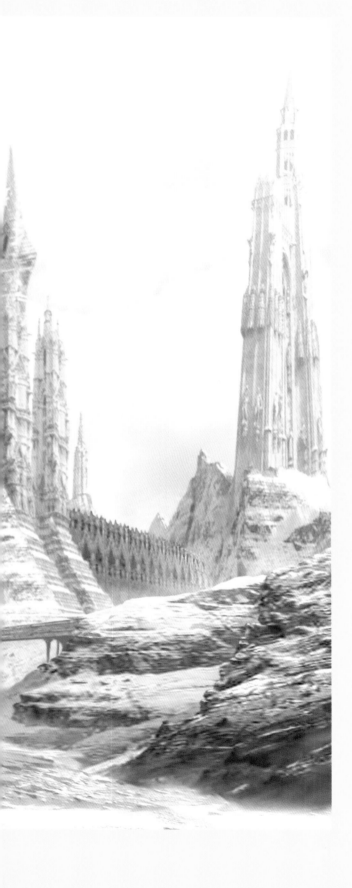

RETURN OF THE ICE CRUSADERS

An advertising campaign for Diesel

Diesel, the well-known fashion brand, asked me to do seven illustrations for their 2004 winter collection to represent the return of the ice crusaders. I had to position the models in a fantasy landscape where they would have lived out their adventure: the quest for the powerful ring belonging to the Evil Emperor of a far-away, frozen planet. These are realistic artworks, even more realistic than I usually do, because the clothes had to be shown clearly so that the customers would be able to recognize them in the stores. A short computer animation made with the Flash program was also created with my ink drawings, illustrating the story more widely on the company's website. The aliens I initially drew seemed too human, and I had to change them a couple of times before I found the right look, but when I finally got it, the art directors sent me an e-mail from London saying 'Max, the aliens are GREAT!!! WE LOVE YOU!!!!'

Below: The white background is useful if you need to add a landscape around the characters in the final artwork, because it can easily be removed with Photoshop. The man on the left is shaking a hairdryer to make the long fair hair (a wig, actually!) of the crusader fly as if he was standing at the top of a mountain. I was thinking about how the girl should hold her spear.

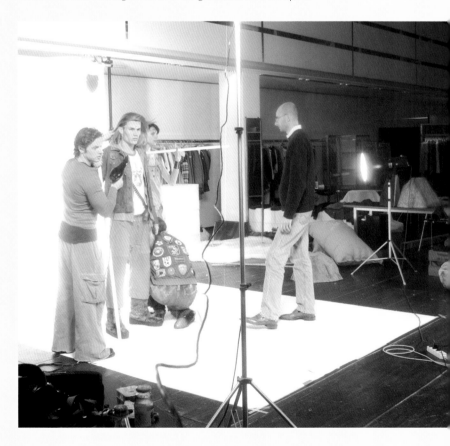

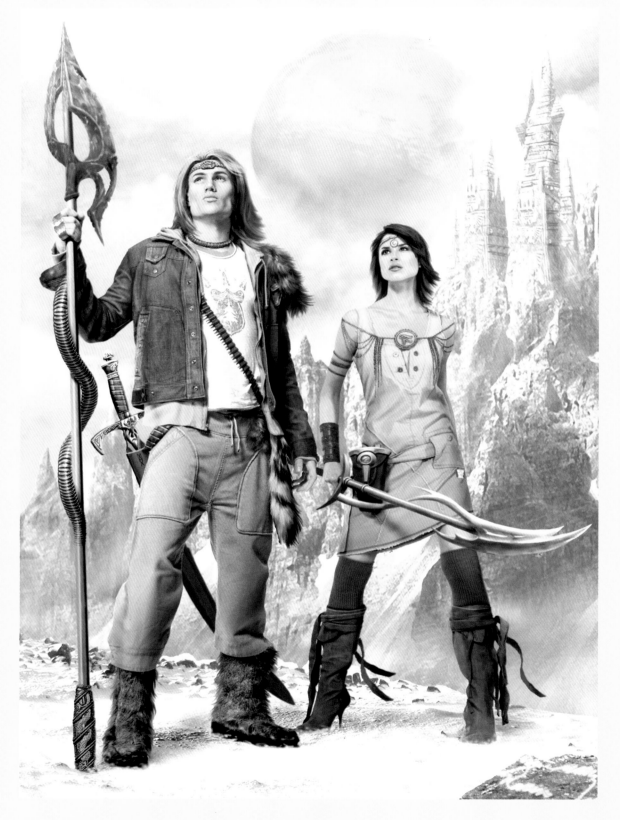

CRUSADERS ALREADY LANDED

Above: Digital, advertisement for Diesel. The starting point for each shot was my preliminary pencil sketches. When we had chosen the clothes and the best posture for the models, we took several photographs of them. I later chose the best ones to use for the illustration. This one was done starting from the clothes you can see on page 37, although I made their physiques more heroic and changed the skin colour to fit the cold environment.

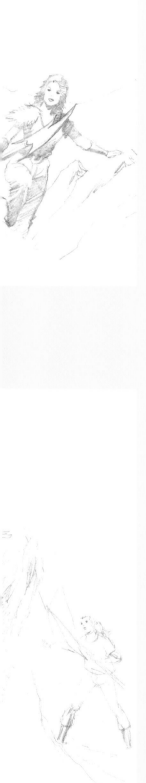

EXPLORERS

Above: Two preliminary sketches for the finished painting **(right).**

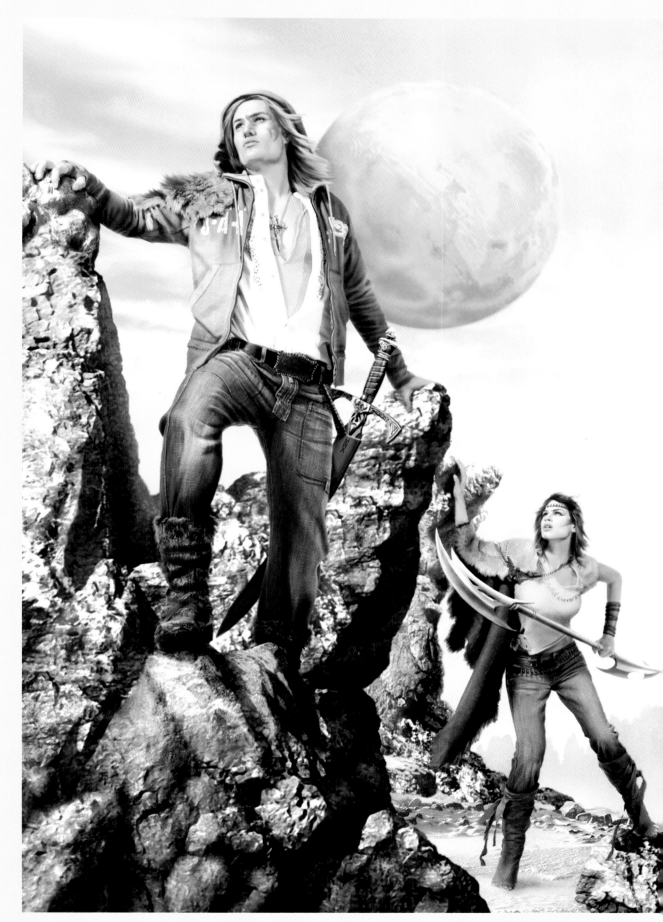

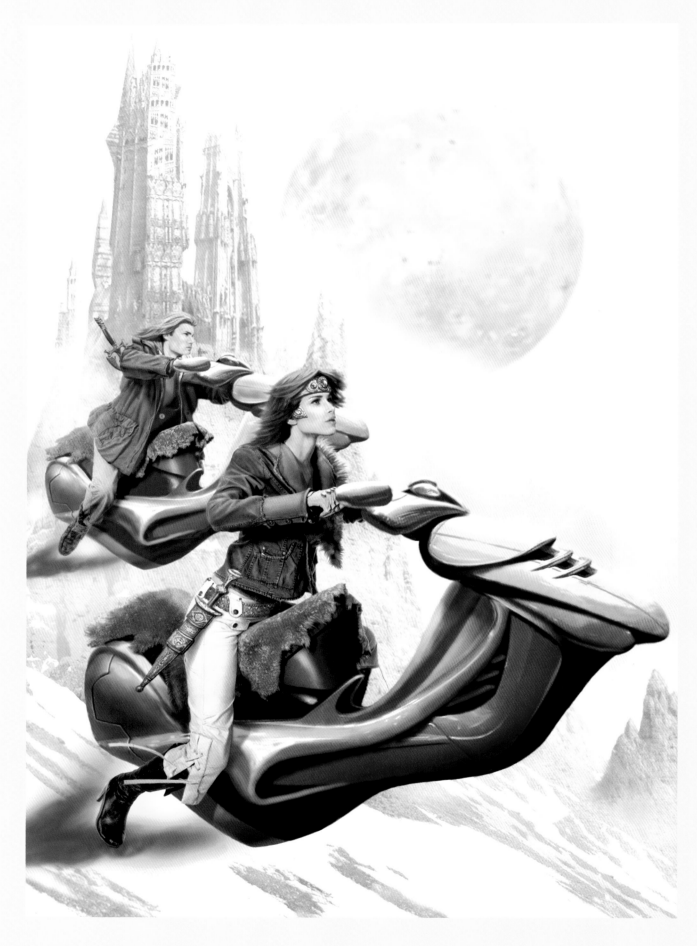

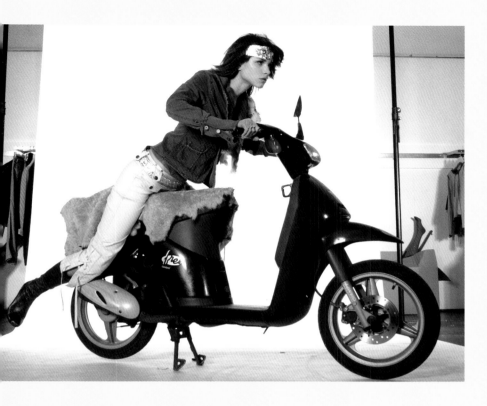

Left: For this illustration I just needed a photograph of the characters riding on ... something! I added the flying craft under them later. In an earlier version, I made the background snow and blue sky, but it didn't work, so I chose shades of red.

CRUSADERS ON FLYING BIKES

Right: The first idea for *Crusaders on Flying Bikes*. We changed the angle of the photograph in the final shot (**left**) because the company needed to show the clothes as clearly as possible. I also gave a different look to the bikes. At first they were quite heavy models but finally they had a lighter body, so they didn't distract the customers' attention from the clothes.

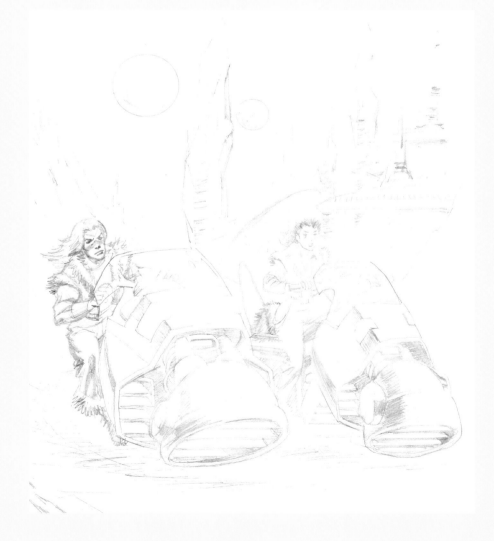

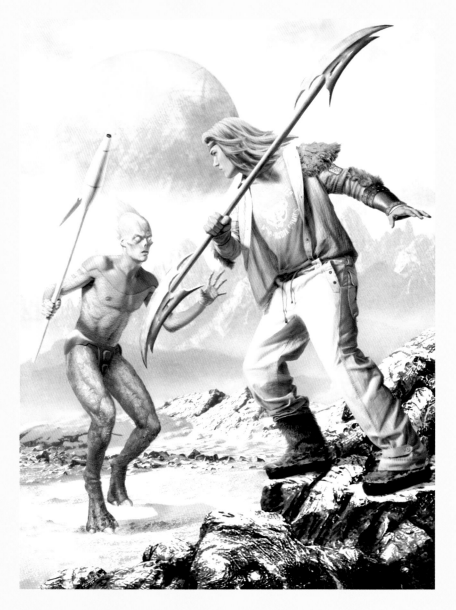

THE CONCLUSION

Right: Digital, advertisement for Diesel The Evil Emperor disappears into the sky after the Crusaders steal the magical ring from him. I chose a circular composition to surround the face in the background. The characters in the lower right corner balance their mass with that of the Emperor himself. Again, I put the characters in the foreground to draw attention to the clothes. This time the composition helped me to give some movement to their bodies, which are turning to see the defeated enemy.

Below: Preliminary pencil sketch for *Fight*.

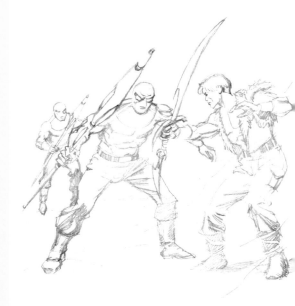

FIGHT

Above: I first drew the aliens wearing trousers and boots, as you can see in the photograph. The art directors didn't like that and I had to make them look more alien. We were all quite pleased with the final result. One of the main problem in all these artworks was giving a dynamic posture to the bodies, because they had to show the details of the clothes, such as labels, seams and buttons.

Right: Reference photograph of two of the main characters involved in *Fight*.

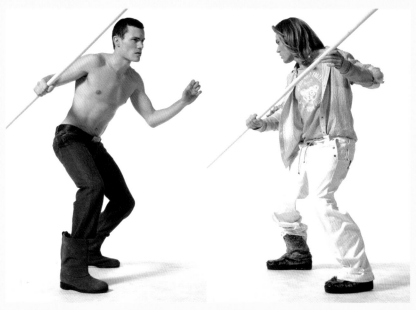

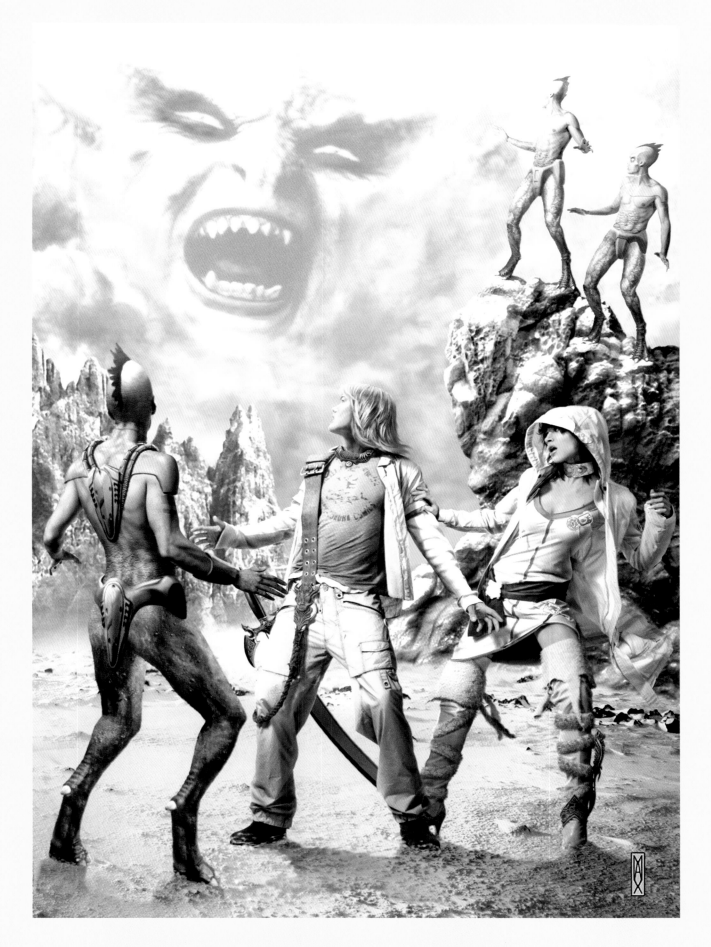

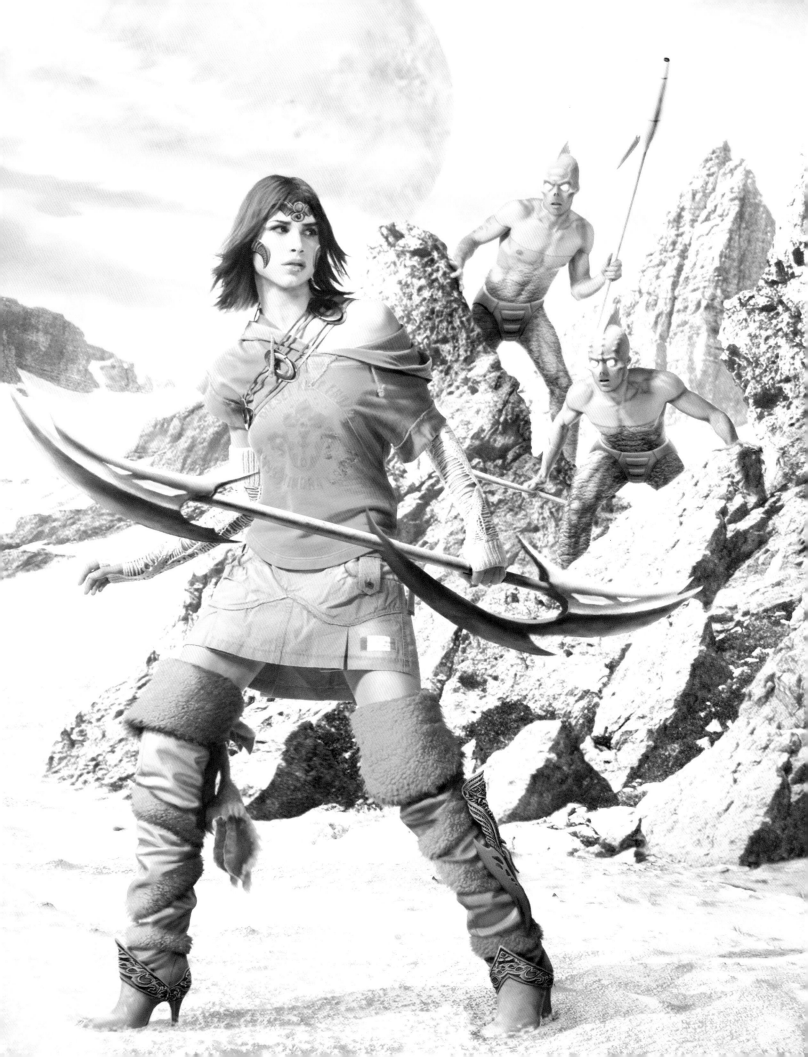

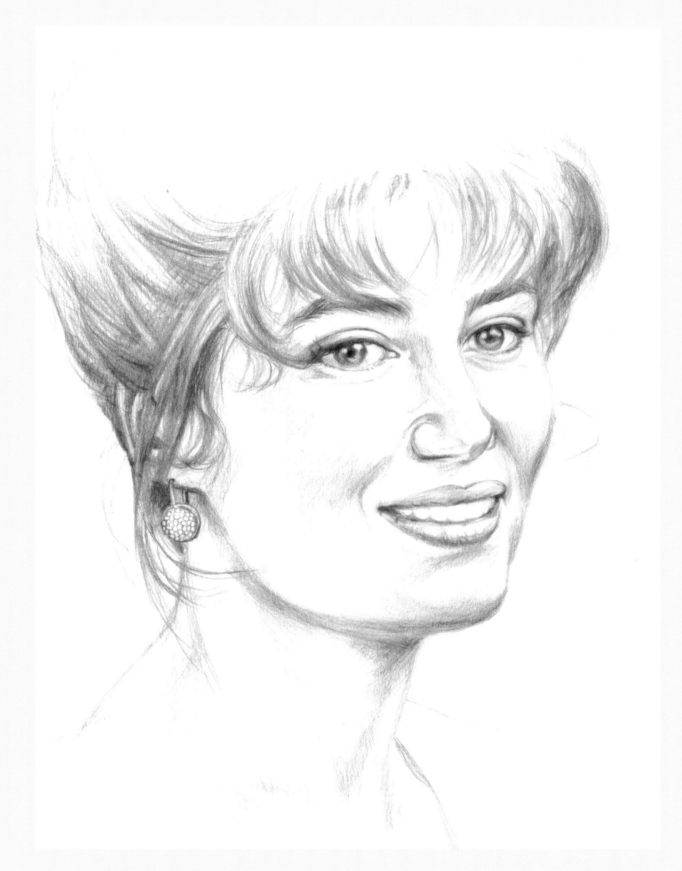

WOMAN EXPLORING

Left: Digital, advertisement for Diesel

PORTRAIT OF ROBERTA

Above: Pencil on paper, 8.5 x 11.5 inches, private work
My wife on her wedding day.

CREATION

When the material on which I will be working has been scanned, I put it all together in a single image and begin, first of all, to work on the composition and matching the colours. Only those who have gone from colouring by hand to colouring electronically can understand the advantages of the latter. The time taken to correct shades is one example. Just think how long it takes to alter the shade of a colour by hand once it has been laid down. Correctly choosing colours before starting a piece of work by hand is undoubtedly an art in itself. Talking to a colleague who still works on canvas and specializes in the fantasy genre, I found out that it is still possible to import a finished piece of work into a computer and make any necessary corrections there. I take the point, but this is like going from London to New York via Cape Town. A pointless diversion, and one to be avoided if possible.

FLAMING ELF

Right: Digital, private work
An image of beauty where the supernatural flaming hair says a lot about the girl's temper. This is one of the very few pictures of mine where I used only a single colour, in all its shades.

PENCIL DRAWING

Below: Pencil on paper, 8.5 x 11 inches

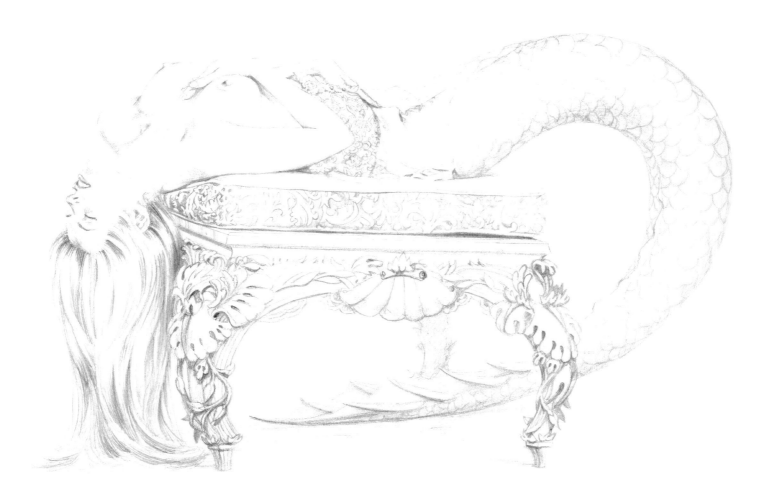

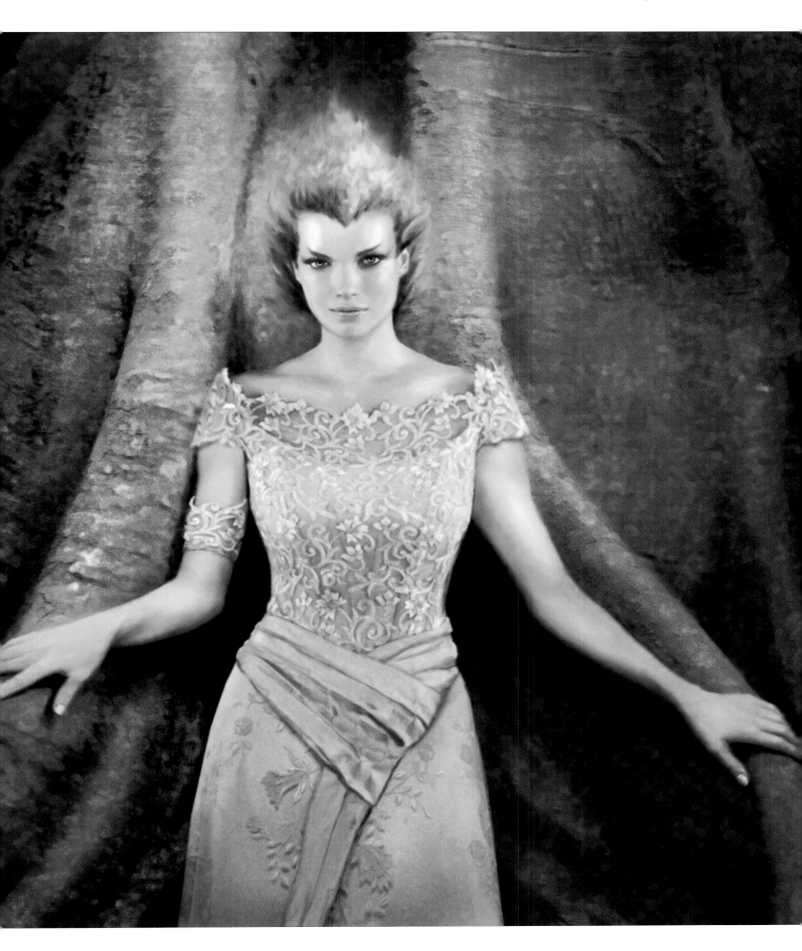

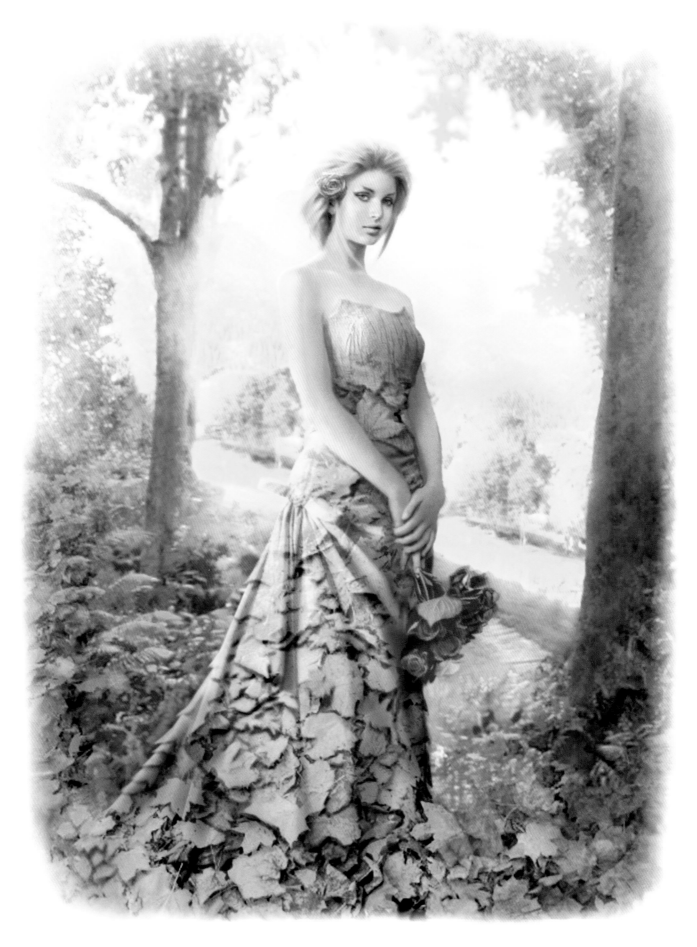

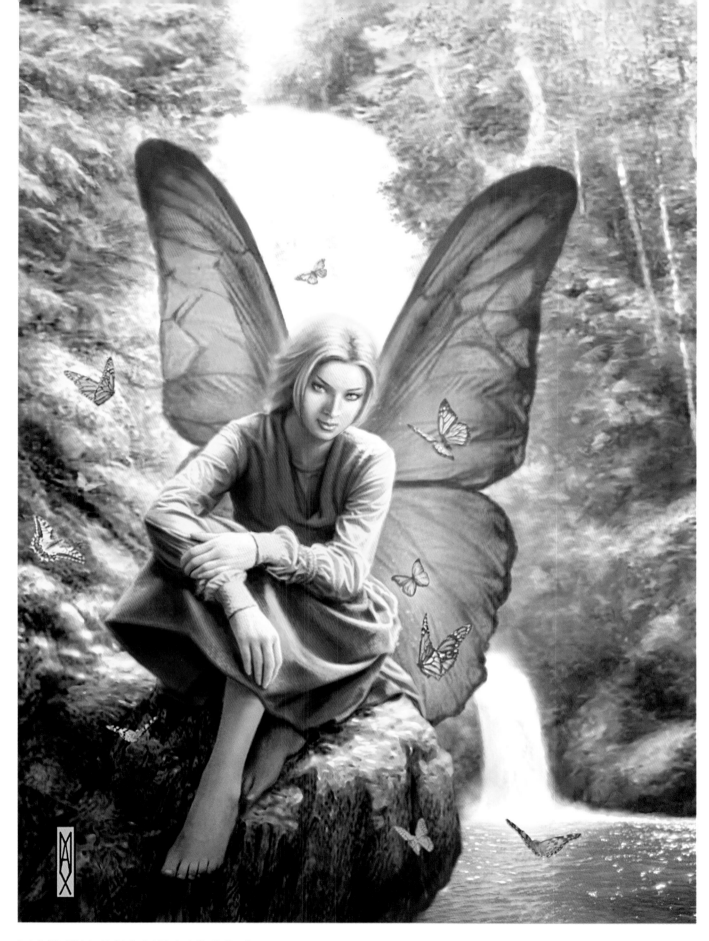

MAIDEN OF THE WOODS

Left: Digital, private work

FAIRY FALLS

Above: Digital, private work

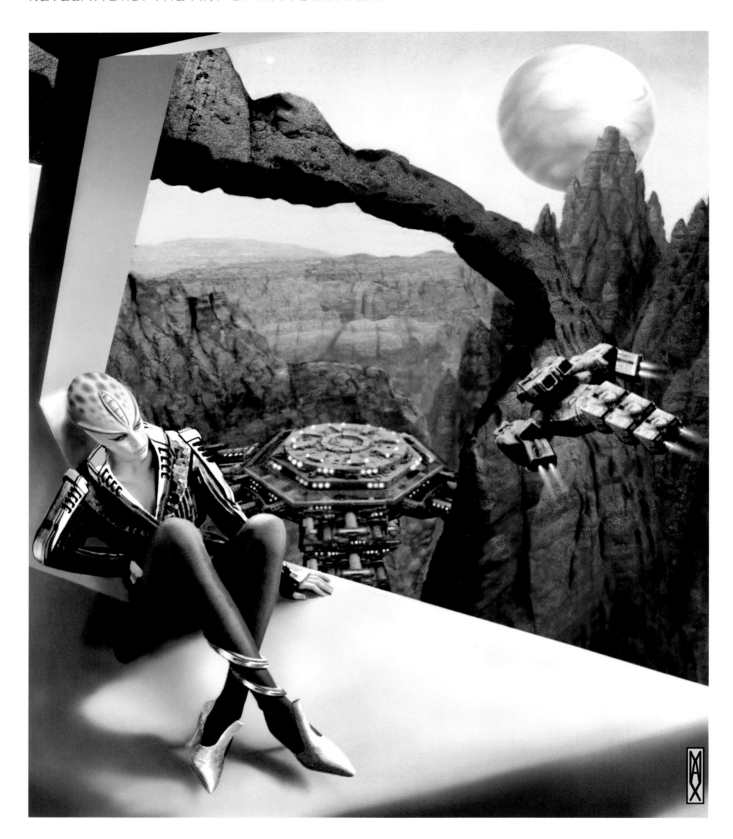

SUNSET ON SHADIR

Above: Digital, private work

A serene sunset elicits the same melancholy in us and
in this inhabitant of an alien planet. I was inspired by
the Rocky Mountains for the background.

I don't want to defend the use of the computer on principle because, clearly, working on screen means giving up other things. More than anything else, I miss having a unique piece that can make an impression on any wall, while an electronic image means you can produce, at most, a few decent posters. Moreover, an illustration produced on a computer has a coldness to it and is nothing compared to the warmth and power of an oil painting. But, as I said, my technique is extremely versatile and enables me, in a matter of seconds, to make changes that, would take days if I had to do them by hand.

PENCIL DRAWING

Below: Pencil on paper, 11 x 8.5 inches

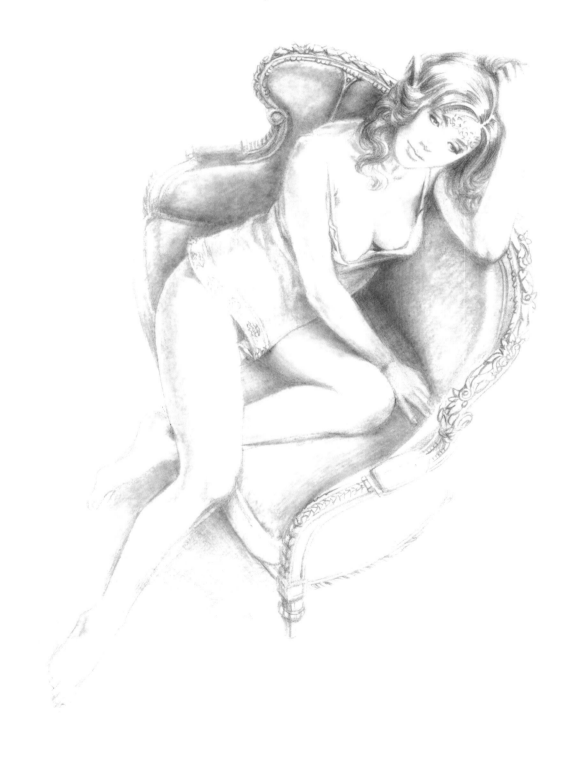

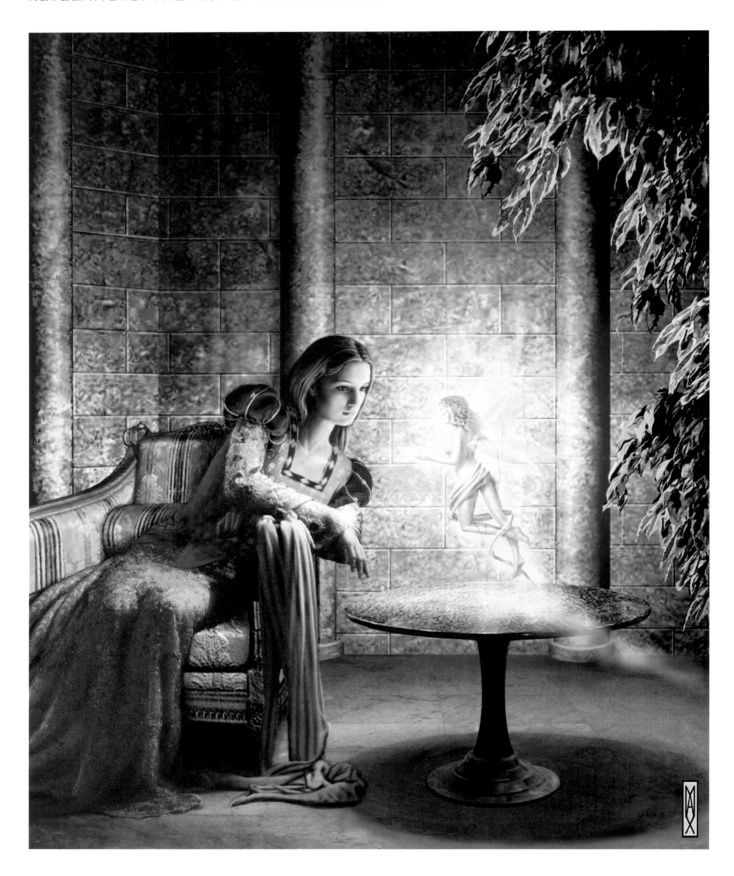

THE ADVISER

Above: Digital, private work

WHITE PRINCESS

Right: Digital, hard cover for B. Eddings's
Tamuli die Schimmernde Stadt, Weltbild

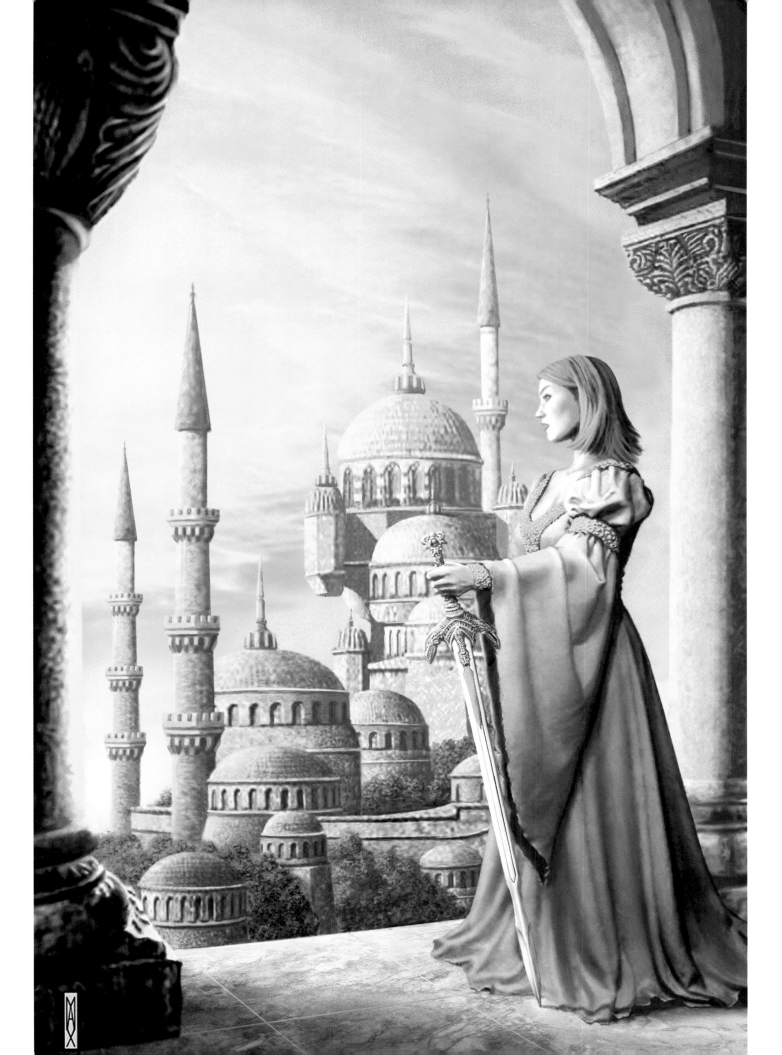

COMPOSITION

Even if you have a basic idea of how you want the end result to look, the process of creation is often uncontrollable and follows a path dictated purely by talent and inspiration. I generally begin with the composition of the image – that is, with the placement of the elements in the illustration (characters, objects, landscapes) on the area I'm working on, in such a way that everything is harmonious to the eye of the observer and so that the viewer's attention is drawn to the elements I want to emphasize – usually the main characters or action. The more elements there are in a drawing, the more important the composition is for the end result. One of the many advantages of using a computer is that, if need be, I can always move the elements of the drawing as I work. An interesting example of composition is *Dragon Flight* (see page 56), in which the dragon, its tail, the trees and hill form a figure-of-eight shape, a double circle that gives a pleasant look to the image. In this case, I didn't know how I was going to develop the balance of the images at the beginning, but, as the work progressed, I became aware that it was naturally organizing itself in that way. It is fascinating to see how creativity can work independently of rationality. I often find this to be the case in my work – I simply follow my intuition, designing as I go. Sometimes the solutions to my problems come to me when I'm half-asleep.

Composition is one element of art that the untrained eye picks up on with difficulty, even if it can detect a satisfying equilibrium in the image it is looking at. An example of triangular composition is represented by *The Final Fight* (see page 57). The subject was a pitched battle between men and ogres, so I had the problem of putting numerous characters together. My solution was to compose a triangular image in which the warrior was placed at the top of the illustration and the ogres to the sides, encircling him. By moving the warrior, the centrepoint of the illustration, to the right, just out of the centre of the drawing, I created a slight imbalance that gives everything a certain energy.

CITIZEN OF THE SEA

Right: Digital, private work

How would a civilization that was born in the sea develop? I imagined the creatures would be sociable and intelligent and sea turtles seemed like a good starting point. The interior of the vehicle was based on the cockpit of a US Space Shuttle.

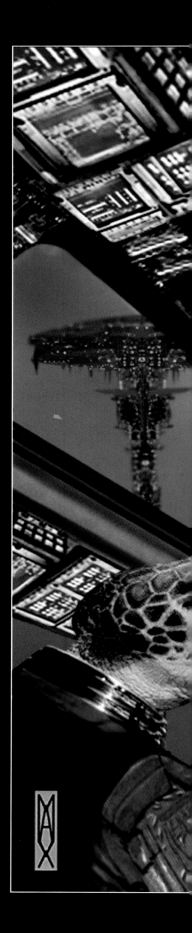

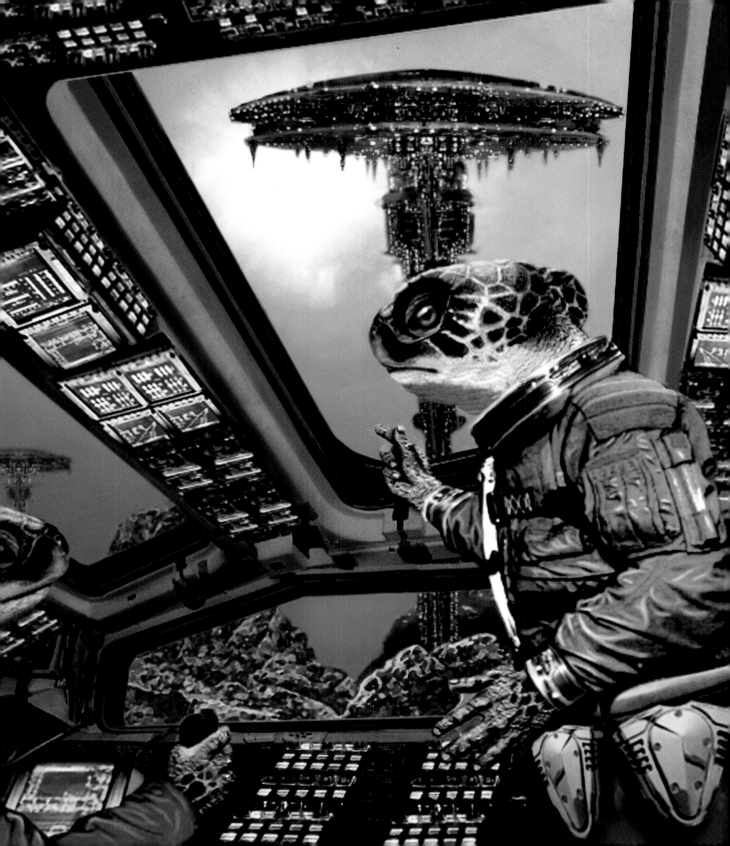

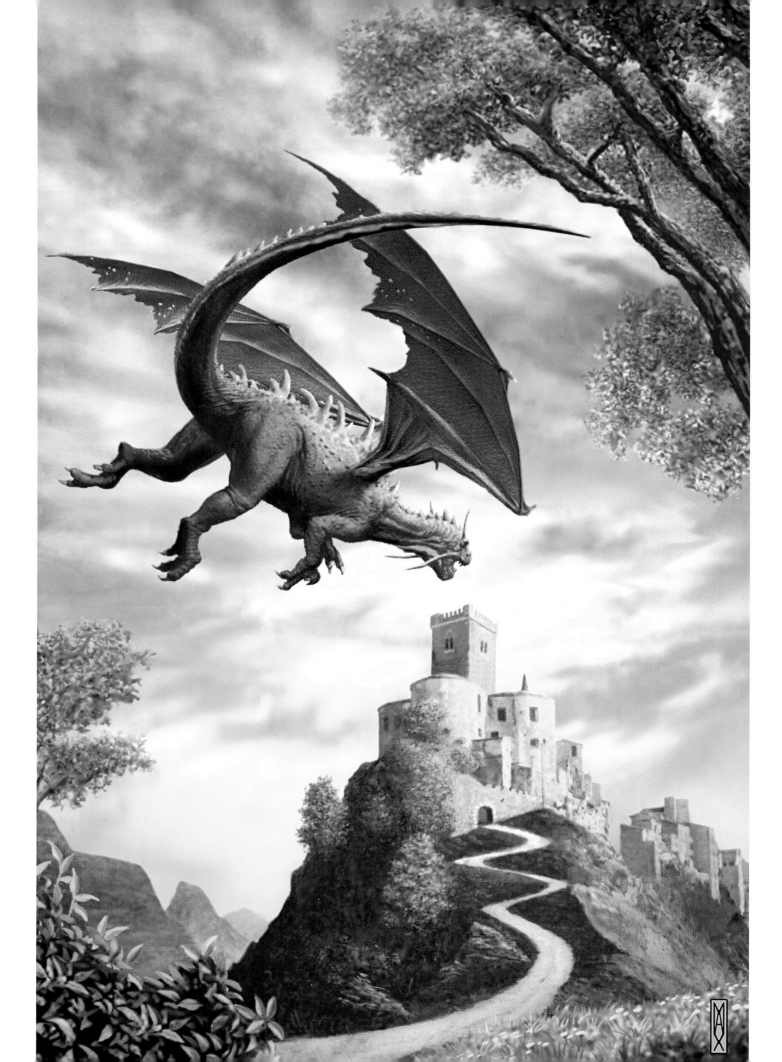

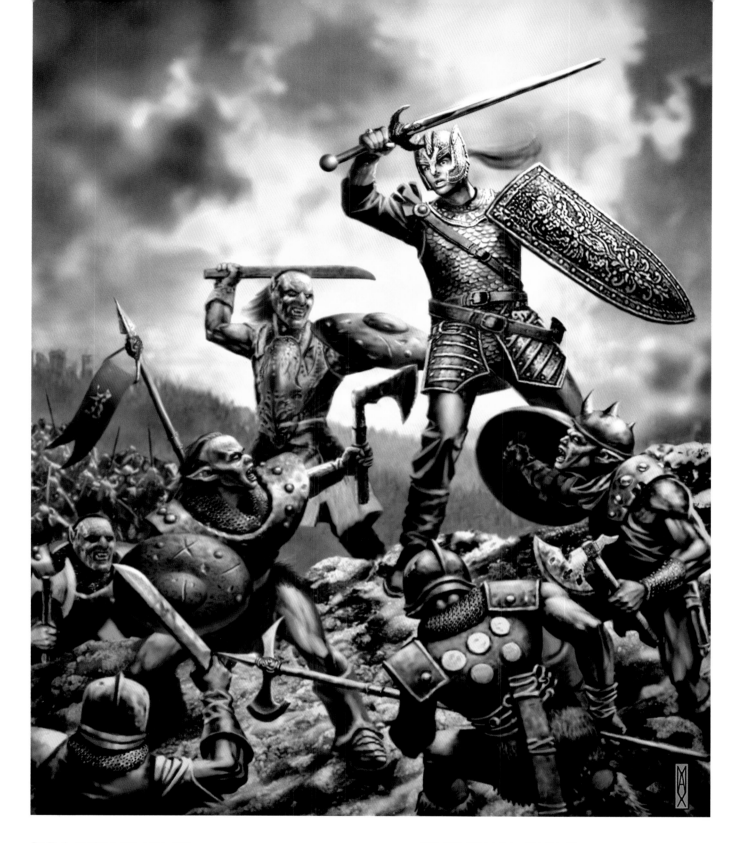

DRAGON FLIGHT

Left: Digital, cover for AST Publisher

The flight of the dragon is a powerful archetype, representing a flight into our subconscious. The dragon symbolizes wisdom and eternity. The dragon has lived for eons and is immortal as our souls are supposed to be. I did this artwork as I'm fascinated by the idea of seeing a dragon flying above my head, his wide shadow hiding the sun and the sound of the wings beating against the wind.

THE FINAL FIGHT

Above: Digital, cover for AST Publisher

I used some models to build the set of this illustration, then I took a photograph to look at for the shadows. But the real problem was balancing the black and whites to give the right emphasis to each figure. The focus of the image is the knight who stands at the apex of the triangular composition, and that is where I also put the main light of the picture.

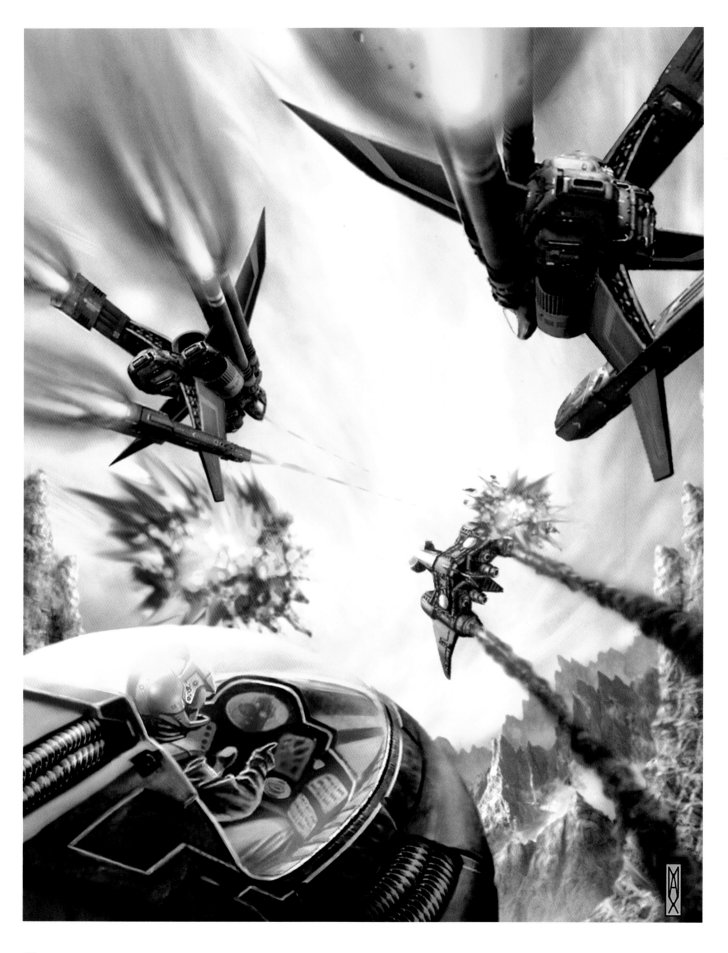

SKY HOUNDS

Left: Digital, private work

I worked hard on the composition of this illustration to create a spiralling effect to convey the feeling of aerial combat, with the various craft performing stunts to shoot down the enemy.

COLOUR

When I have decided in principle how the illustration will be composed, I begin to analyse the choice of colours. Many people have said that the colours I use in my work are pleasant, and studying the great artists of the past was certainly a great help to me in this respect. Their solutions have a universal value and can be used in all types of work, from science fiction to fantasy. I enjoy matching various shades of red and green, as in *Young Galadriel* and *Emerald Guard*, but I also often combine purples and blues, sometimes with reds, as can be seen in *Megara*, *Death Field*, *Goliath*

NEVERENDING YEARS First try

Right: Digital

This was the first attempt at *Neverending Years*, the cover for Clifford Simak's book *City*. The art director didn't like it, however, and I had to think of something else.

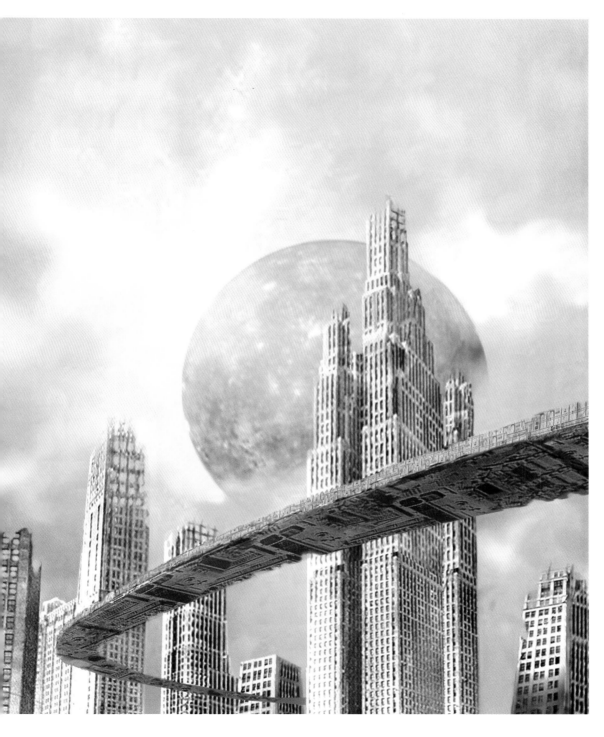

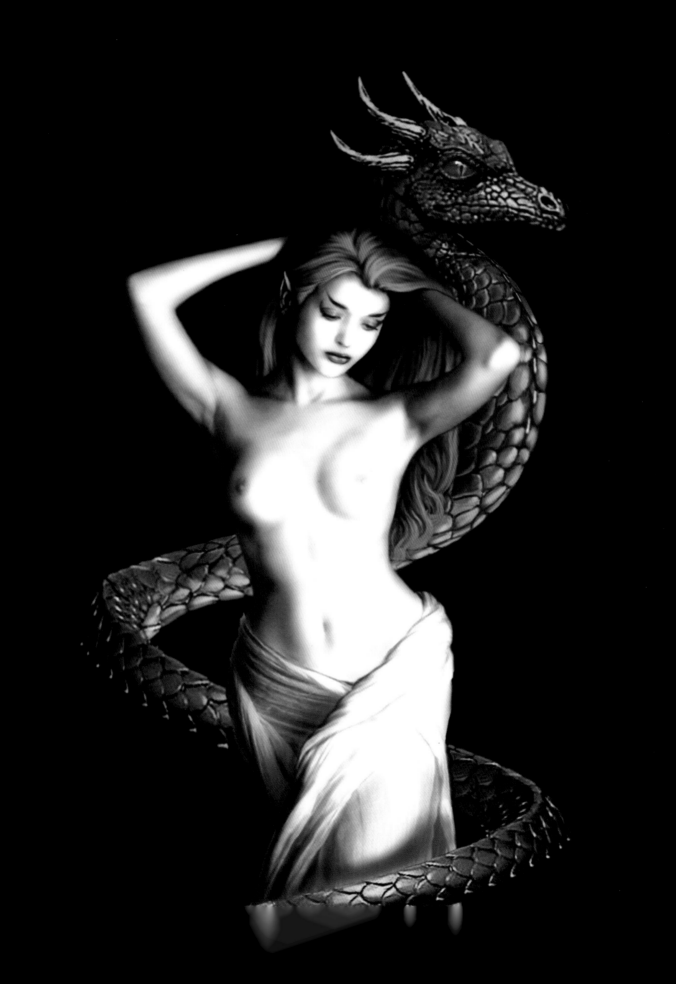

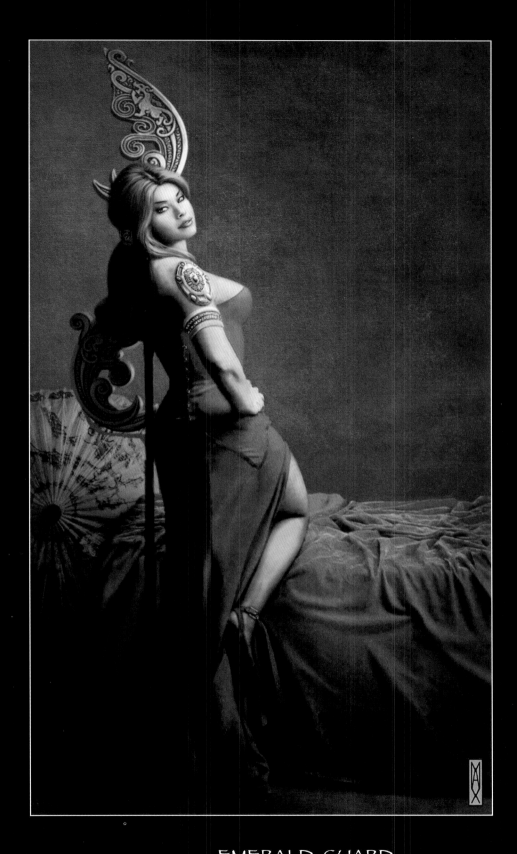

YOUNG GALADRIEL

Left: Digital, cover for Eura Editoriale

EMERALD GUARD

Above: Digital, private work

A beautiful woman, even if she is a warrior, can overcome the viewer with nothing more than a look. I wanted to show refined seduction when I began to draw this.

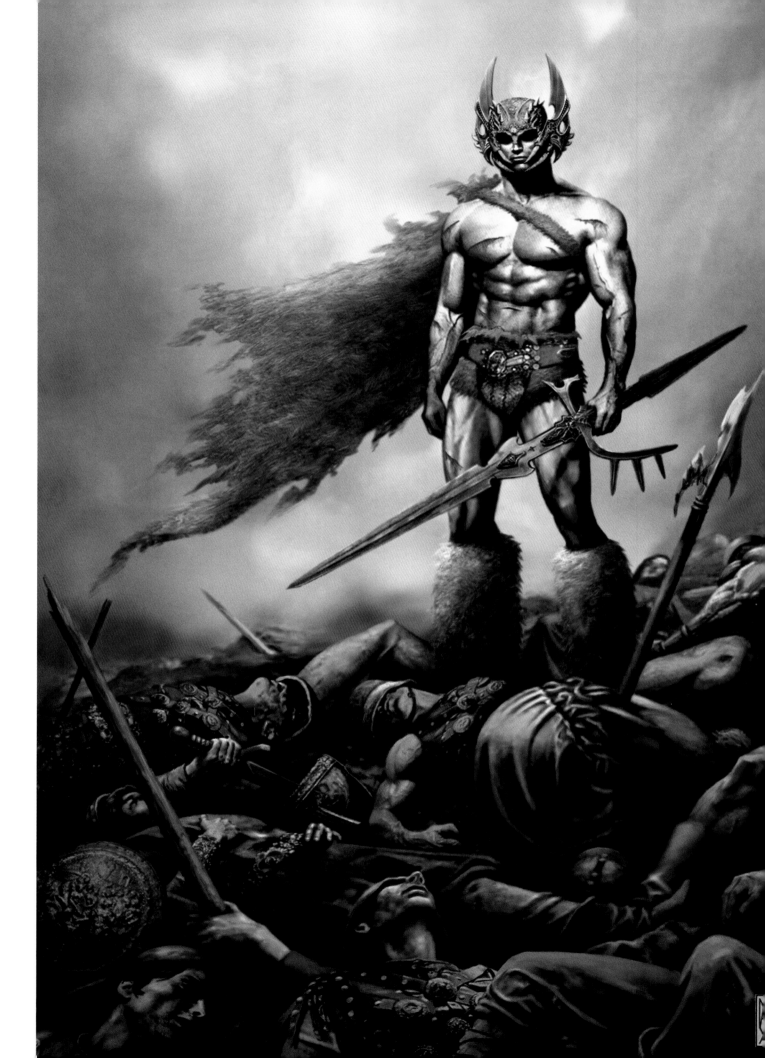

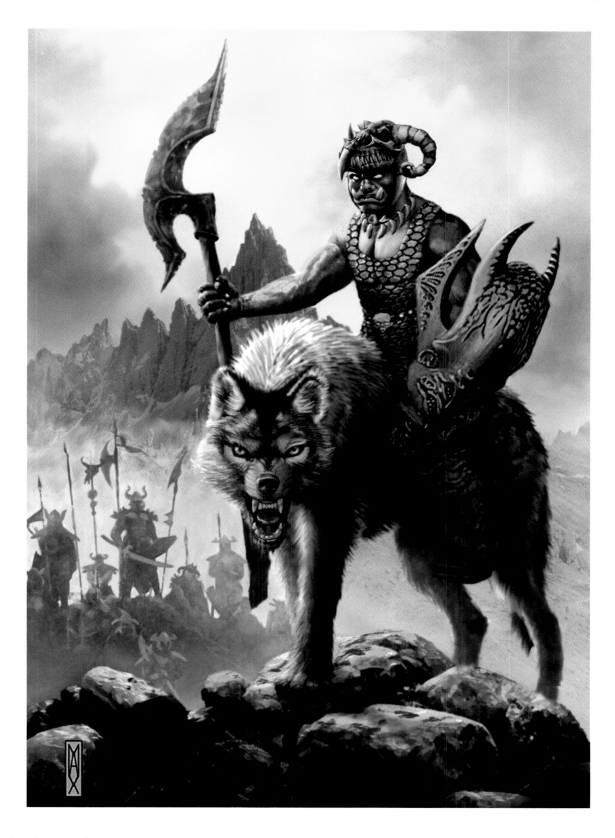

DEATH FIELD

Left: Digital, cover for AST Publisher

I like illustrating the tales of heroes and their conquests in imaginary lands.
Though he may not always behave like a gentleman, the hero's strength, wit and
resourcefulness help him triumph over his enemies, no matter how many or how
strong they are.

MOUNTAIN ORCS

Above: Digital, cover for AST Publisher

and *Elfic Vessel*. Each colour has a specific emotional value. For example, if I want to portray a battle scene, I usually prefer to use red, which transmits anger, with blue to create a strong but effective contrast that serves to heighten the drama of the image. However, with pin-ups I tend to employ less strongly contrasting combinations, which prove more intriguing for the viewer. The computer is a great help, even when it comes to choosing colours, enabling me to change them in a moment and to select shades with extreme precision. The correct choice of colours is vital for the visual impact of an image, and I count myself extremely fortunate to be able to call on tools that once upon a time were not available for this purpose. Selecting the right colours is a process that I take very seriously and do with great care. If there are several elements in an image, each one must have colours that attract the attention. An example of this is *Star Core* (see page 18): there are numerous colours in play here, but the combinations work successfully. In terms of colour, I resolved this illustration by lightly toning the blue of the sky with yellow. The resulting colour, a shade veering towards green, links the yellow of the stars with the strong green of the trees in the foreground.

An object never has its own colour: it depends on the light and colours that surround it. There are almost always several sources of light, but when we are outside in the open air, the main source of light is generally yellowish because of the sun. A blue coat, for example, will reflect some of the sun's light, and the skin of the wearer will no longer be a light pink but rather a purple colour in the areas where the blue light from the coat falls on it. It is a continuous and absorbing challenge for an artist because the task is not to reproduce reality – this can be done well enough with a decent camera – but to interpret it with emotion, personal taste and experience, thereby creating a piece of work that has an intrinsic additional meaning, a degree of universal value. For example, a portrait of a beautiful nude woman can't just be anatomically correct and erotic; it must also be symbolic of grace and balance. Similarly, an ogre can become the essence of evil and disharmony. The viewer only rarely perceives these meanings consciously, but on an emotional level the message is always received. Through the imagery, the illustrator speaks of themselves, and the emotion they have put into the drawing is always visible. It is for this reason that, at times, technically perfect work can leave the viewer feeling somewhat indifferent; in these cases the artist perhaps had little to say and merely used technique to complete the illustration. For this reason, when I study the works of the great masters, I like to try to understand what they were thinking: I don't just read their biographies, therefore; I also let their paintings tell me about them.

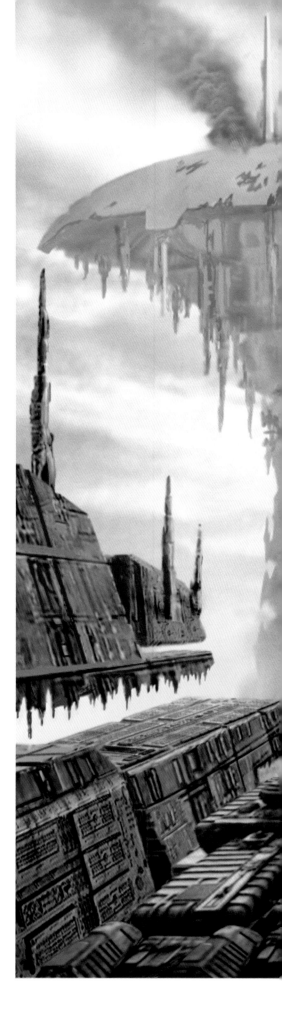

MEGARA

Right: Digital, cover for *Fantasy & Science-Fiction Magazine* and *Galaxies*

A futuristic city after a bombardment, with the fire that is still burning reflected in the sky. I like the enormous scale of the ships and the amount of detail in this image, which took me a couple of weeks to complete.

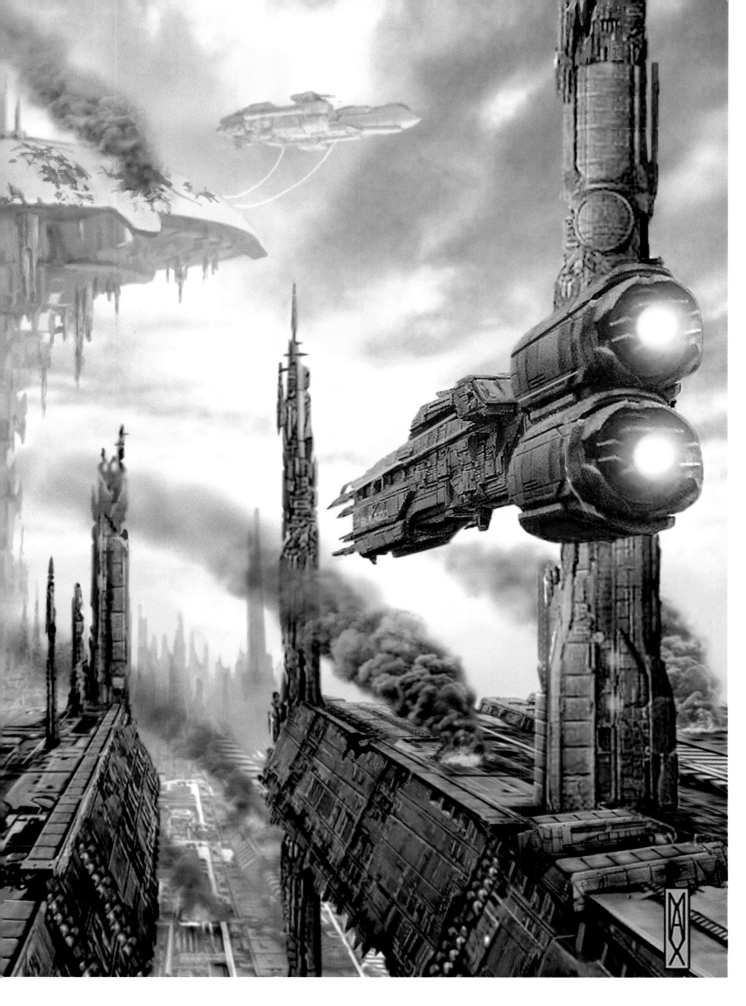

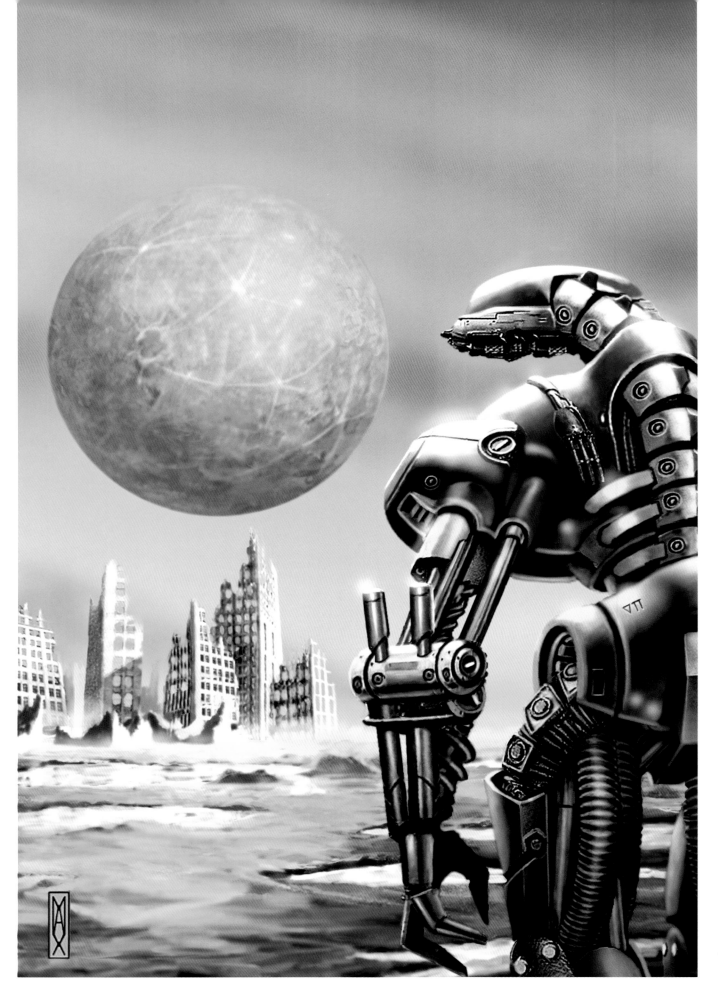

NEVERENDING YEARS

Left: Digital, cover for Editrice Nord and *Galaxies*

This was drawn as a cover for *City*, the novel by Clifford Simak. I initially drew a sky full of clouds, but the art director said he needed something more symbolic and less realistic. I followed his advice, and when I saw the result, I had to admit he was right.

YELLOW SUBMARINE

Below: Digital, illustration for online *Yorick Fantasy Magazine*

The submarine had to be yellow, but the colour clashed with the background, and I decided to turn it a bit more green. Nobody seemed to have any complaints.

LIGHT

The use of light and shade has a decisive effect on the success of an illustration, and the effective use of light can often make all the difference to a piece of art. Having worked for many years on black–and–white comics, I have developed a good feeling for the use of light, and this is obviously also useful when I am doing drawings in colour. Without the correct light, colours are relatively useless. I often see pieces of work with good colour combinations but that lack the right light – the final effect being irretrievably flat. The end result is cartoonish. In my illustrations light often plays a decisive role, even if I still feel that I have much to learn about it. When a picture fascinates me, I realize that it is always because of the way in which the artist has employed light. Degas's ballerinas or some of the interiors by the Flemish masters are exemplary in this respect – light envelopes them as if it were a living presence, giving the painting a soul. I've learned to place the majority of light on the main character, in particular on the face, decreasing the light as I go down the body. In this way the face, usually the part of the anatomy on which the greatest attention is focused, receives the majority of the light. Ingres often worked in this way, and many of my pin-ups use his work as a reference in terms of the use of light. With this in mind, the facility offered by Photoshop to work on every detail independently, using the layers and selections, acts as an amazing tool: at any moment I can alter the intensity of light on any single object in the illustration until I achieve the desired effect. In *The Final Fight* (see page 57) I used a fair amount of background light around the main character, attaining the desired effect in the process.

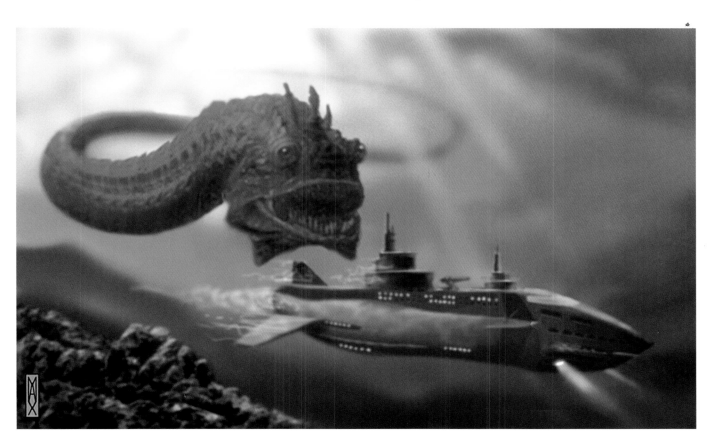

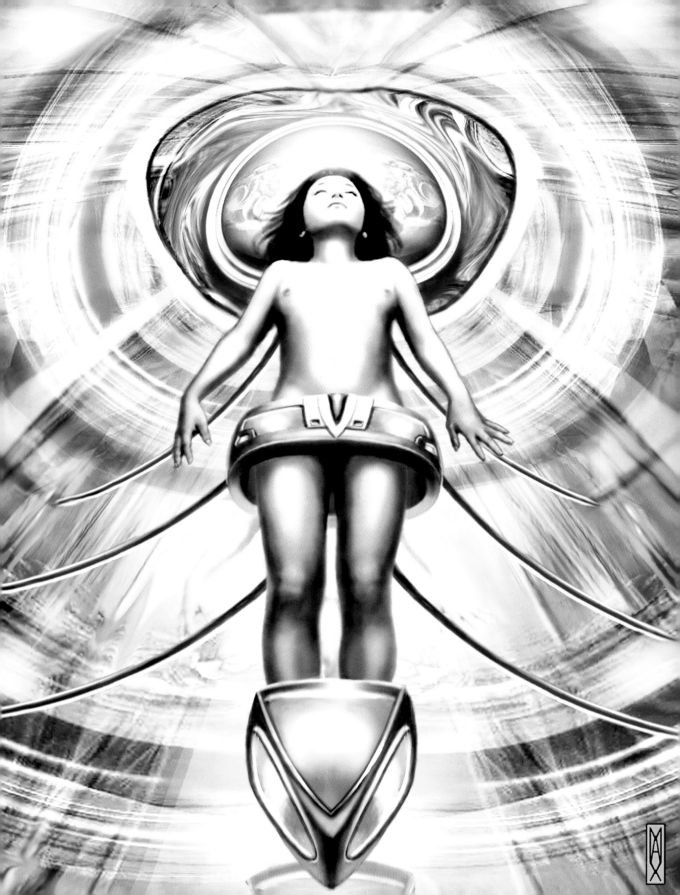

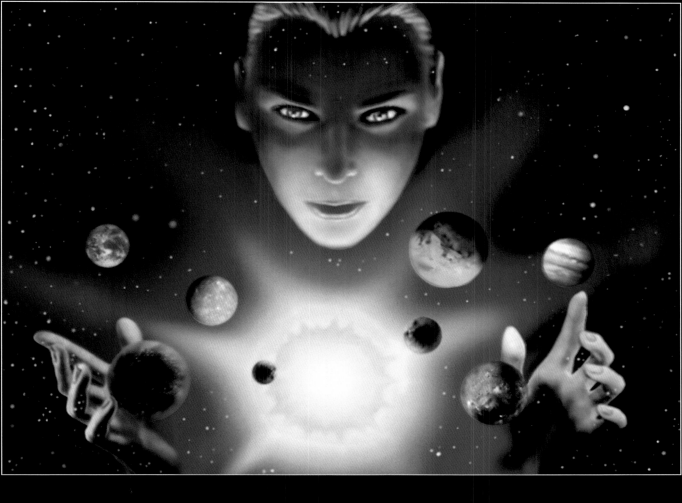

CREATION

Above: Digital, private work

I was inspired by the words in the Bible, 'Let there be light … ', but in my mind God has to look like a woman, as she is the bringer of fertility.

GOLIATH

Left: Digital, cover for *Goliath*, Solid Books

I was given a chapter of the book to read and decided to show the young woman melding her consciousness with a futuristic computer. This struck me as a powerful and appealing image, a metaphorical return to the universal mother.

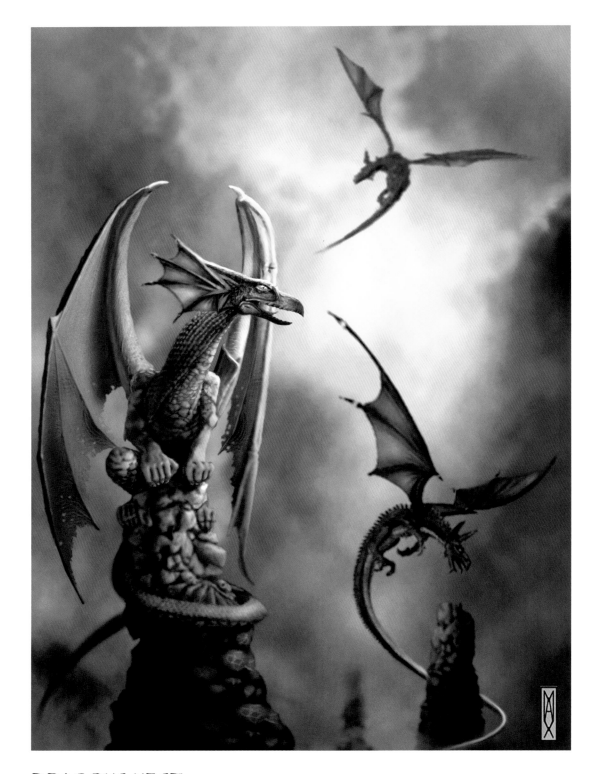

DRAGONS NEST

Above: Digital, cover for Kate Forsyth's *Die verwunshenen Türme*
Blanvalet and for AST Publisher

I imagined a place on the top of the world where dragons could live alone. Amid the western mountains mist dwell the fearful Grey Dragons. Keeping their ancient secrets, they hide from the curiosity of the little people. The publisher saturated the reds and the contrast in the sky in order to make the cover more visible in the bookshops. I was surprised at first but then admitted that the final result was impressive.

DEATH CARRIER

Below: Digital, private work

In the near future peace will still have to be maintained through force. I like the colours, and I like the atmosphere of looming war and the lights in the sky that reflect on the sea. I used the US Air Force F22 as the model for the jet in the foreground.

THE DETAILS

The most tedious job is refining the image – correcting all the smears or blemishes and clearly defining the figures. I have a passion, almost an obsession, with anatomy: I have drawn bodies in motion since I was a child. I believe that studying the human body is of primary importance for an artist, and I attempt to do it in as much depth as I possibly can. I continually observe those around me to understand how to draw from all angles and, when I'm talking with someone, I sometimes lose the thread of the conversation because I'm so busy studying the lines of their face, hands or other part of their body. My aim – unattainable – is to memorize the human body in every possible position. Working in the comic industry for such a long time has refined my knowledge of anatomy, and this is one of the strong points of my drawings. Many good illustrators lack a solid anatomical knowledge, and this is something that weakens their work, even if they compensate for it with a good use of colour.

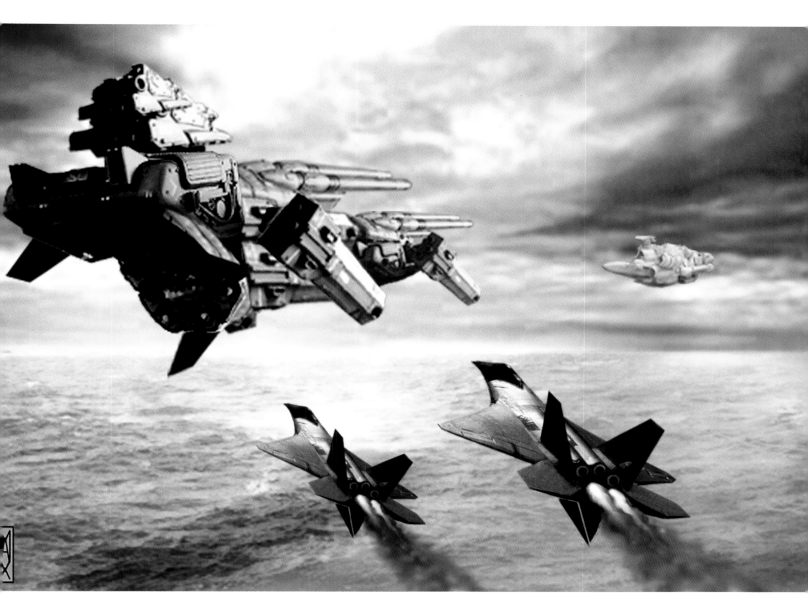

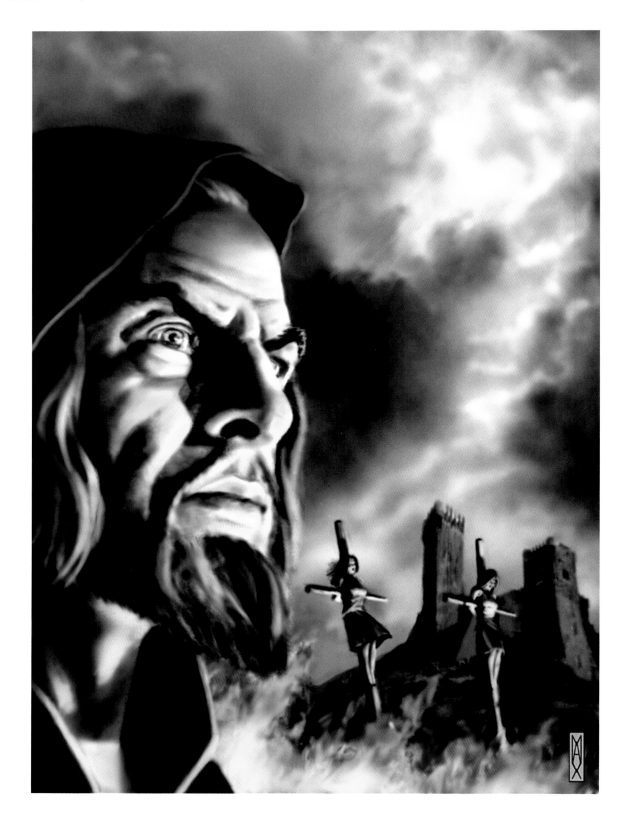

EYMERICH

Above: Digital, cover for *Eymerich*, Solid Books

The fire of hell on earth will bring those women, accused of sorcery by the inquisitor Eymerich, to the paradise waiting above. I depicted the clouds almost like stairs, which may take their souls to heaven.

ELFIC VESSEL

Right: Digital, private work

I'm often looking for a feeling of wonder and grandeur in my artwork. Here is a good example of what I'm talking about. I think an illustration should be suspended in time and talk to the soul about unknown worlds where magic still exists.

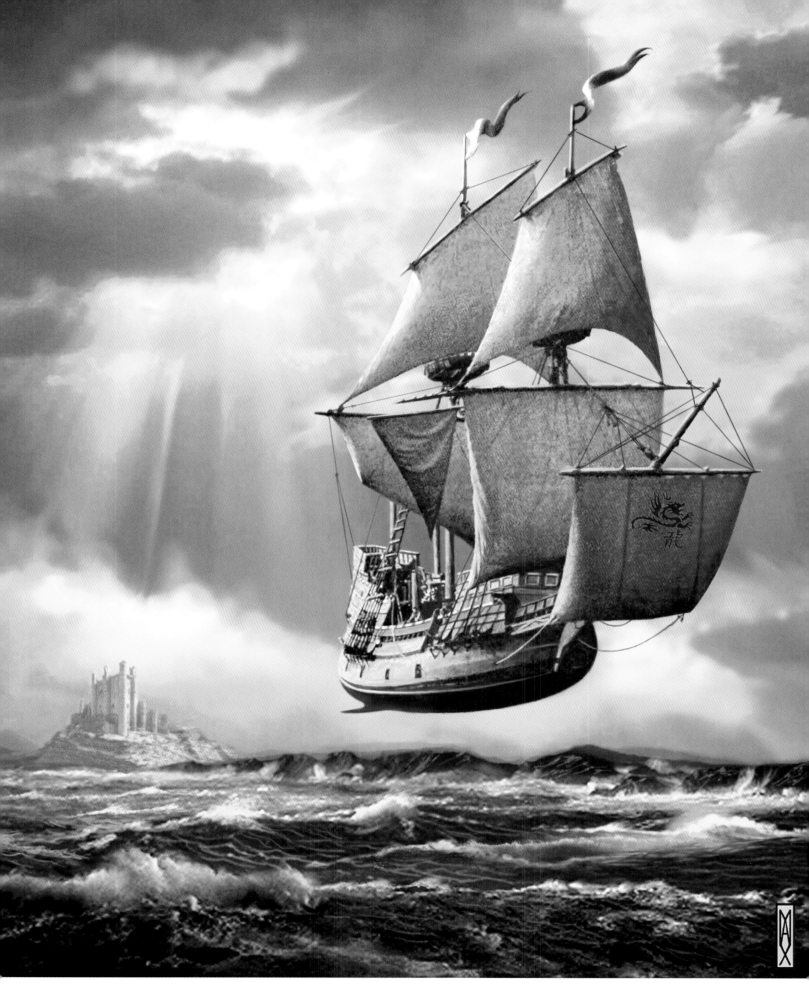

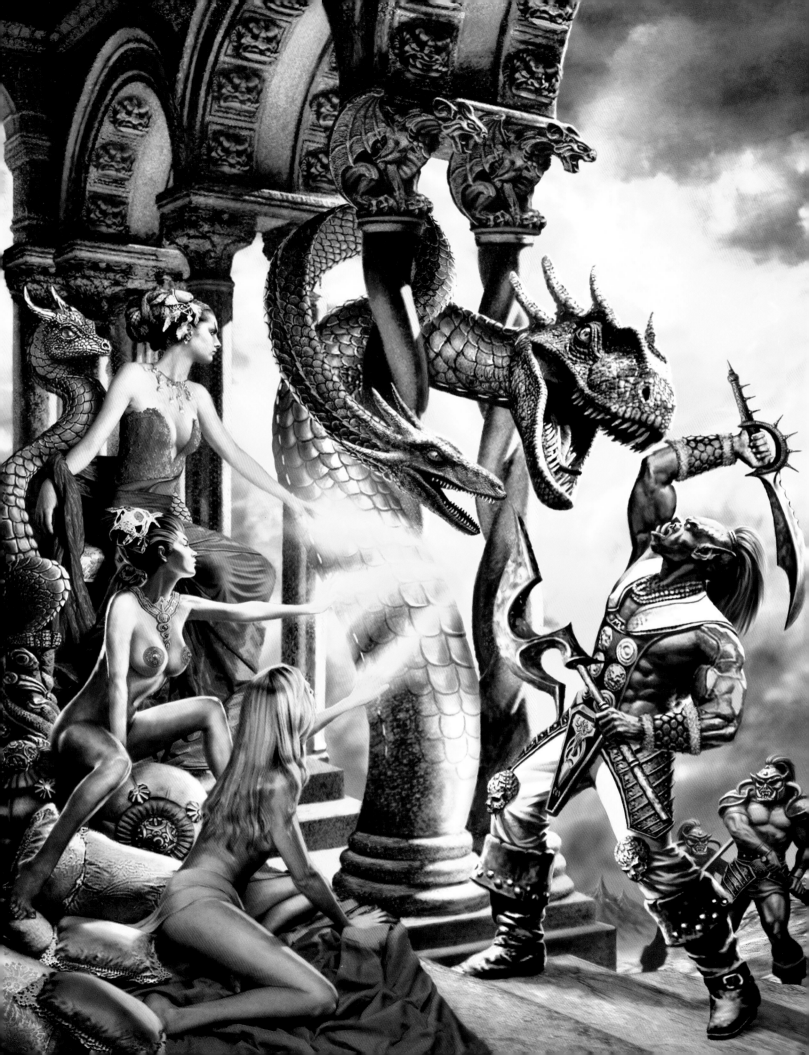

THE SORCERESS CASTLE

Left: The first version of this picture had a castle in the background. I eliminated it after I finished the illustration because it was becoming confused with the other figures and details. I also changed the sky, turning it from red to this shade of yellow ochre. The hardest task was painting all the scales on the dragons and finding the right colours for the cushions and the skin of the characters. When you draw so many objects in the same picture you have to decide on the main light source and make all the different colours reflect it.

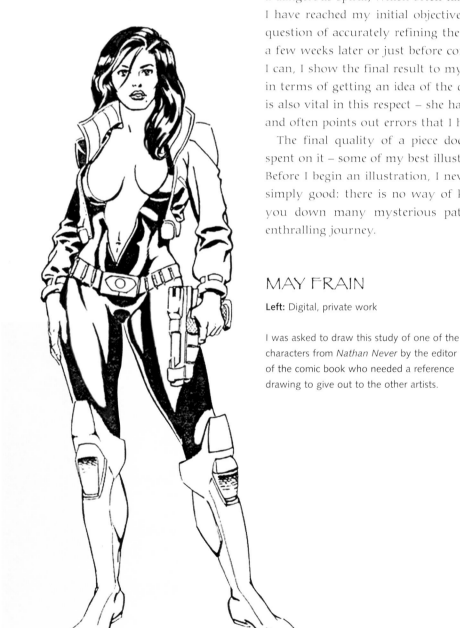

THE SEPARATION

Once this phase is finished the work is almost done, and I put it aside and don't look at it for a couple of days. You lose your ability to be critical if you spend too much time on the same drawing and start believing you have produced works of art, even when there are major errors present – errors that are noticeable only after some time. For this reason I like working on more than one image at a time. In this way, I am able to be critical without needing to take long breaks. I achieve my best results when I get hold of a drawing again several months after completing it, without having looked at it in the meantime.

Deciding when an illustration is finally complete is a real problem for an artist. Leonardo da Vinci never stopped refining the *Mona Lisa*. You always believe you can improve an image further, but the search for perfection is a dangerous spiral, which often takes you nowhere. I generally stop when I have reached my initial objective. From that moment on it is merely a question of accurately refining the colours and contrast, work I might do a few weeks later or just before consigning a piece to the publisher. When I can, I show the final result to my colleagues – for me the only valid test in terms of getting an idea of the quality of my work. My wife's opinion is also vital in this respect – she has an excellent appreciation of aesthetics and often points out errors that I haven't seen.

The final quality of a piece does not depend on the amount of time spent on it – some of my best illustrations were done in two or three days. Before I begin an illustration, I never know if it's going to be excellent or simply good: there is no way of knowing. The process of creation takes you down many mysterious paths, and each time it is a tiring but enthralling journey.

MAY FRAIN

Left: Digital, private work

I was asked to draw this study of one of the characters from *Nathan Never* by the editor of the comic book who needed a reference drawing to give out to the other artists.

FANTASY OR SCIENCE FICTION?

My first love is science fiction, but when I was about ten years old I also began to be interested in the fantasy genre. I think that the first fantasy novel I read was *The Sword of Shannara* by Terry Brooks, a book full of the magnificent colour images by the Hildebrandt brothers. I still remember the magical atmosphere that pervaded them, and I used to spend hours with my eyes glued to the pages. To be honest, at that time, all my artistic energy went into drawing superheroes; colour illustrations seemed, technically, very far off. Now that my taste is slightly more refined, fantasy, perhaps even more than science fiction, seems an enormous universe, whose roots go as far back in time as mankind itself and which explains our base instincts, from the mythology of ancient civilizations right up to the great contemporary literary sagas. Artists have an embarrassment of choice in this area, in terms of both subjects and costumes, and they can have fun mixing fashions from different ages.

DRAGON'S WRATH

Right: Digital, cover for *Terre di Oscuria*

I like drawing awe-inspiring dragons, and most of all I like giving them the breath of life, which means natural movements and correct anatomies. I studied the dinosaur's body structure to create this piece, and I'm quite pleased with the result. I put the warrior woman on top of the rocks to give her a fighting chance to defeat the giant beast.

KILLER HUNTERS

Left: Digital, cover for *Segretissimo*, Arnoldo Mondadori Editore

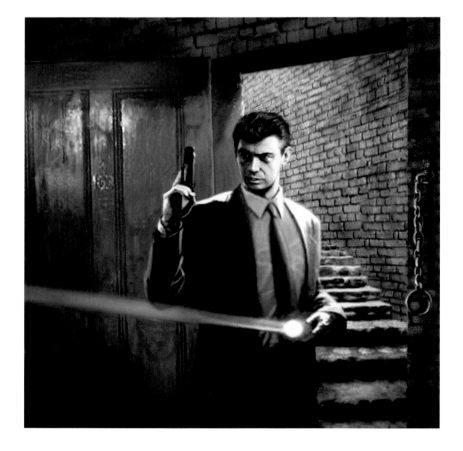

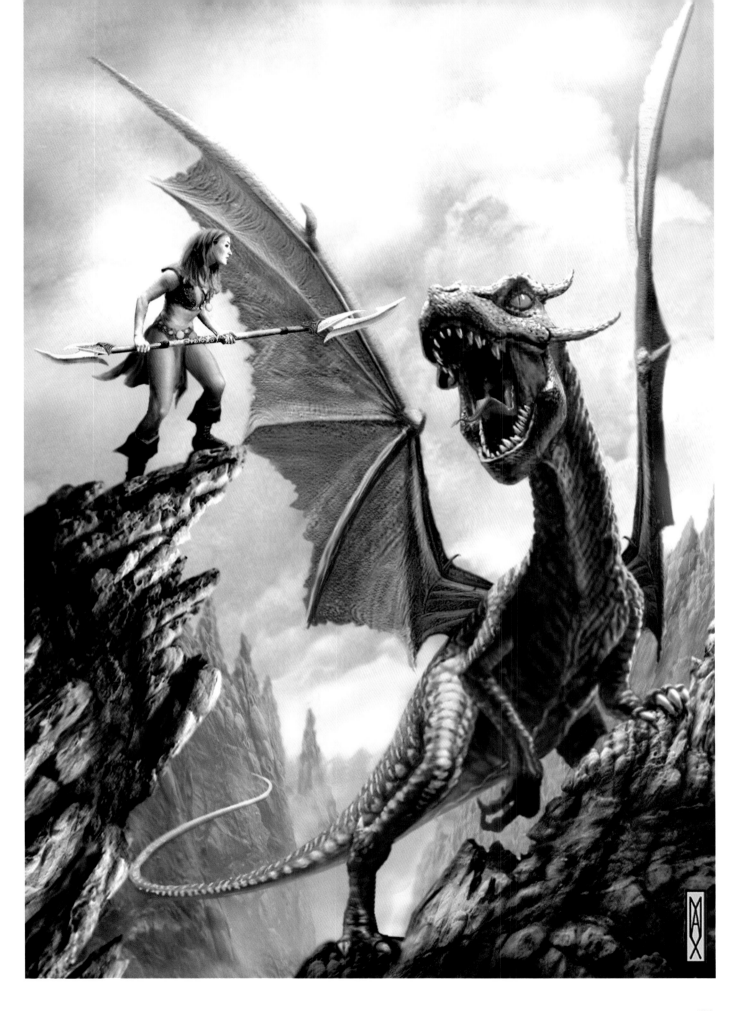

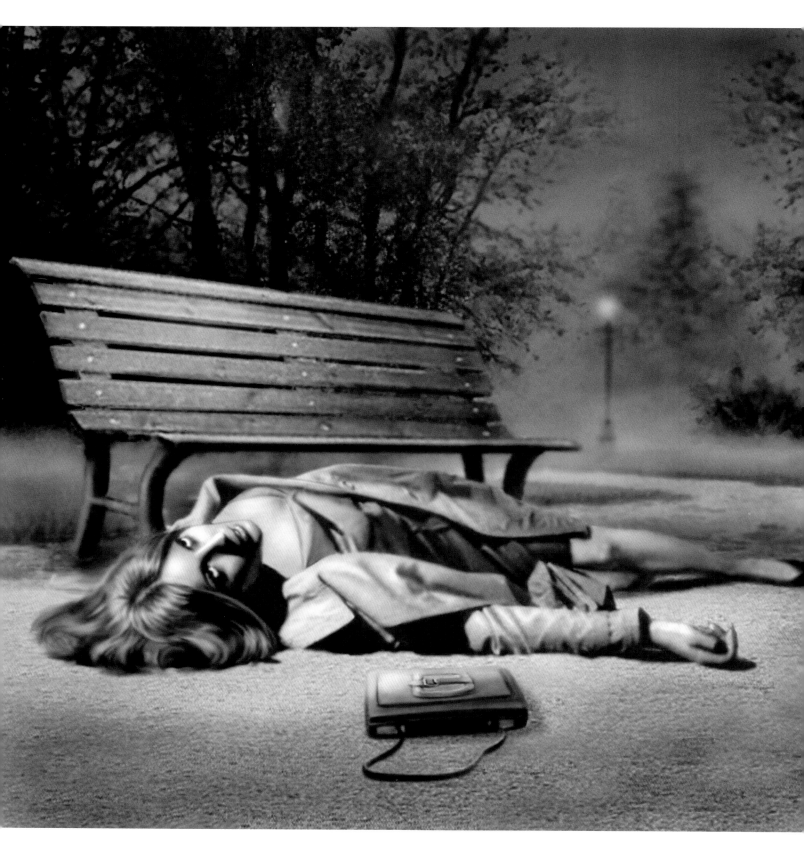

VIOLENT BIG CITY

Above: Digital, cover for *I Gialli*, Arnoldo Mondadori Editore

The ground level viewpoint I chose is quite uncommon, but it allowed me to show clearly the face of a young woman killed in a park. She looks astonished, asking why she has been murdered.

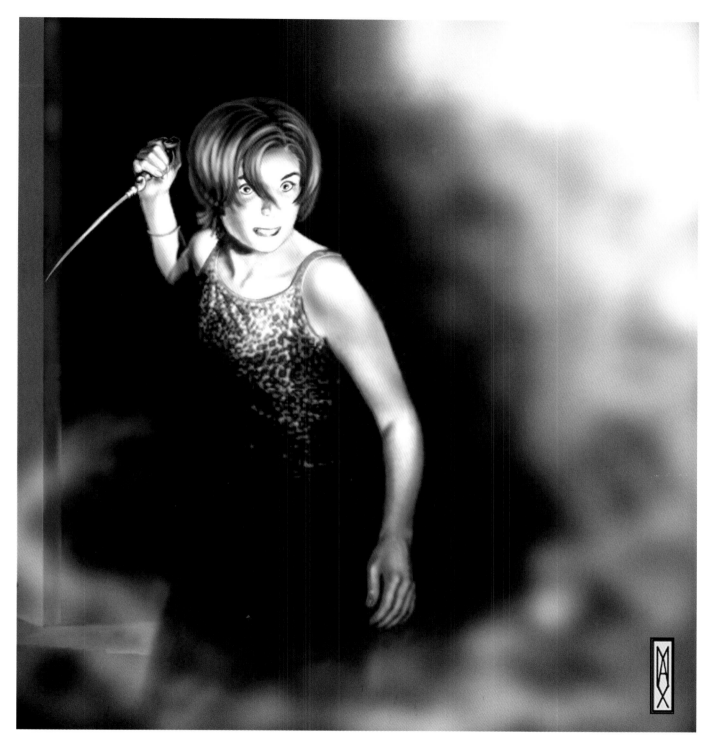

KILLING FOG

Above: Digital, private work

I love all fantasy genres, including horror and thrillers, and professionals should always try to vary their work as much as possible to keep up with the changing tastes of the public. However, among all the possibilities that the market offers, it is almost obligatory for artists in this field to dedicate themselves to the fantasy genre. Fantasy has such a wide market because the themes it deals with are universal and easily comprehensible to the public. In contrast, science fiction has always had a more dedicated, smaller, mainly male, fan-base, because technology and exploration of far away planets seems to attract a largely male public. The prevalence of

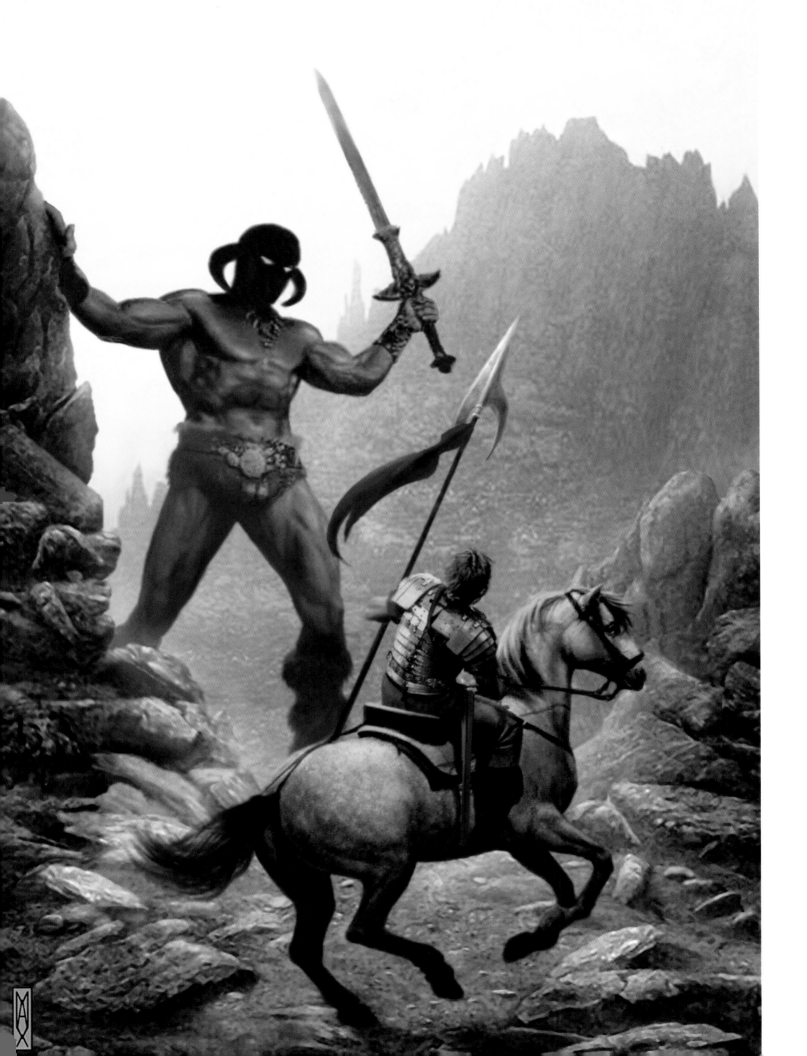

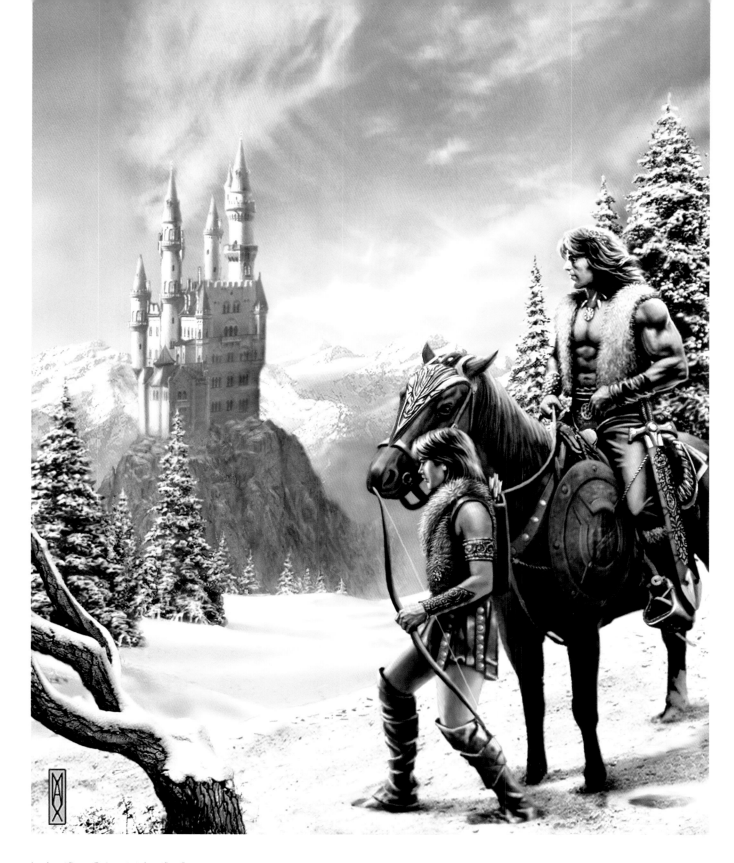

LAND OF GIANTS

Left: Digital, cover for AST Publisher

I had some difficulty with the colours here. I couldn't decide on the dominant one, until I chose the greens and yellows, which finally matched well. A touch of red here and there gives more life to the picture. The possibility of easily changing colours with the computer really helped me this time.

GOING BACK HOME

Above: Digital, inside illustration for *Il ritorno di Conan d'Ausonia*, Yorick Fantasy Magazine

This was the first time I had to draw snow. I tried to capture the atmosphere of a bright, windy day, with the blues of the sky reflecting on the soft white surface. The young man with the bow is Conan's son.

fantasy does not bother me though. When I was younger, science fiction gave me the chance to travel in space through my drawings, but, as I've got older, I have begun to sense a profound coldness in this genre. Because it is so concentrated on science and making alien worlds and societies believable, I find that it generally fails to explore the many different facets of the human mind.

Creating extraordinary technologies and amazing space ships is enjoyable – it is like being a child again – but fantasy is something quite different. I consider it a much more mature genre, only superficially is it a distraction for the mind. When I work on a fantasy illustration I feel deeply involved, I touch the deepest parts of my soul, and I draw with a different impetus. I can delve right into the human mind, to the light and dark there, and putting it down on paper is exhilarating. For example, putting women and mythological beasts together creates a strong erotic charge in itself – primitive power and sex are an explosive mixture. Putting yourself in the shoes of a warrior taking on a giant, as in *Land of Giants*, is a challenge that engages me in every respect. If you stop to think for a moment, you will see that in fantasy mythology every race symbolizes a different human theme or characteristic. Elves can be seen to represent our connection with nature, dwarfs our invention and labour, and ogres our more destructive and violent instincts, while magicians signify human wisdom. These characteristics make it possible to represent humans in all their guises. Once upon a time painters drew on classical mythology to analyse the human mind more deeply. Nowadays, illustrators turn to fantasy, which explores ancient myths in new ways.

The continual search for new means of expression for my creativity led me to bring together my passions – fantasy and science fiction – in a single comic book. This is how *Endora* came about, a story that unites the two genres and that represents a graphically challenging project because it is in colour and every single image is a mini-illustration. I enjoy creating distinctive worlds in which my characters can roam. I am trying to create a wide-ranging story, a kind of saga, in which I can put all my abilities, narrative and graphic, to the test.

Unfortunately, the continual search for new slices of the market has pushed many fantasy editors towards producing covers for their books that no longer include the typical narrative elements of the genre, such as dragons, ogres, elves and so on. To attract new readers, the current tendency is to produce landscapes or single objects, such as swords, helmets or towers, which may have some symbolic meaning. I don't get much out of jobs such as these, and, when I can, I prefer to stay in the mainstream, approaching editors who still use illustrations to tell stories and present characters rather than just suggest an idea.

HAUNTED HOUSE

Right: Digital, private work

The ghost of a young child is a silhouette that takes shapes under the light of a full moon. Who knows the reason for her restless wandering? What is she looking for? A lonely forgotten soul, forever young and trapped by the boundaries of time and space. I always feel complete empathy for the illustrations when I'm drawing and felt slightly uncomfortable doing this one.

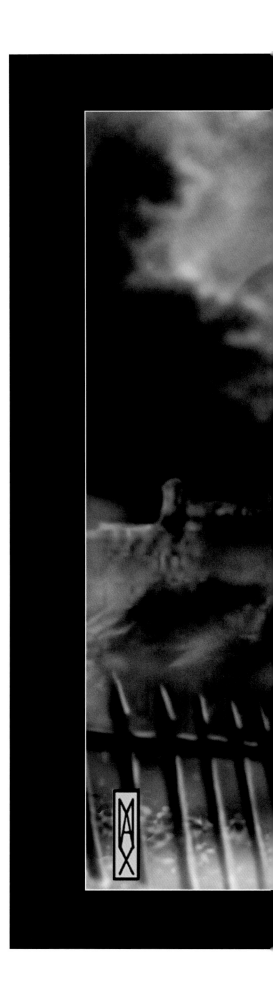

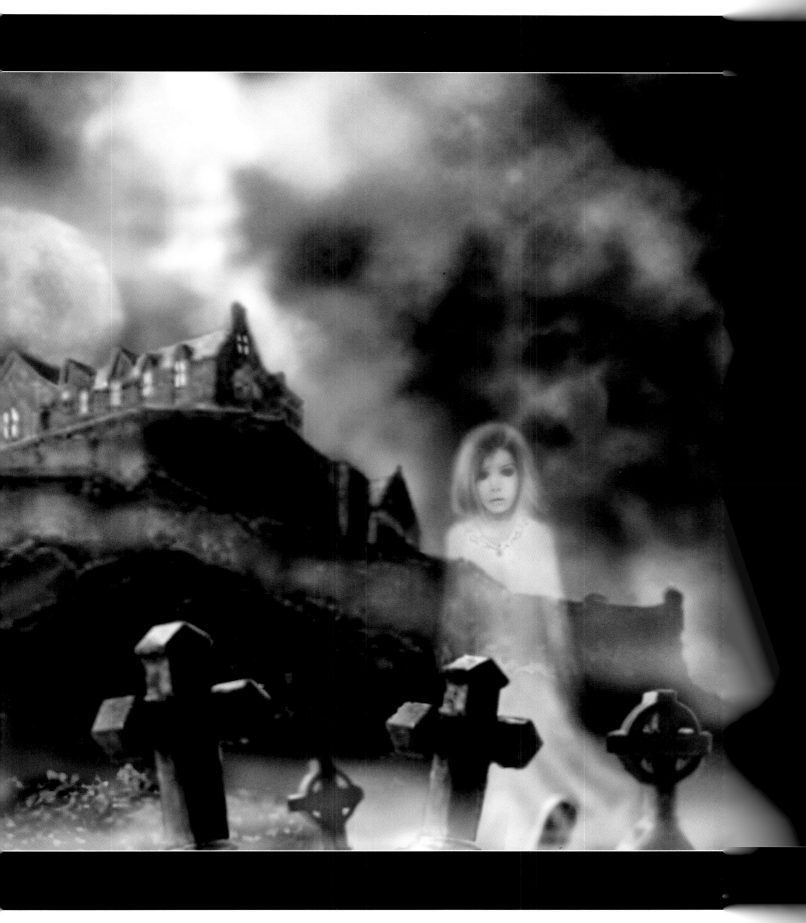

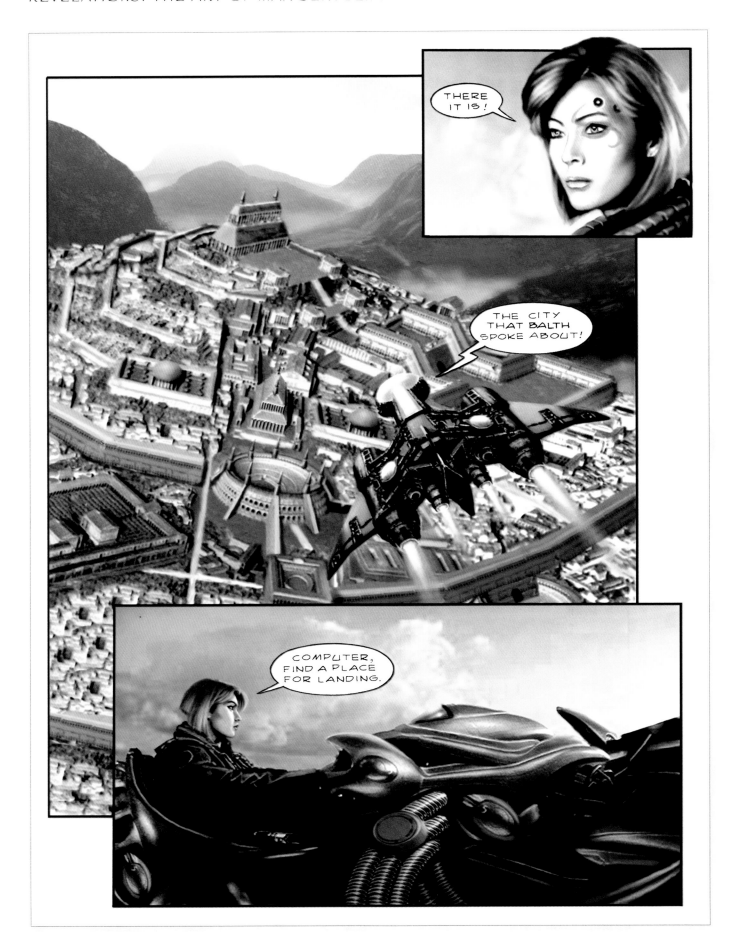

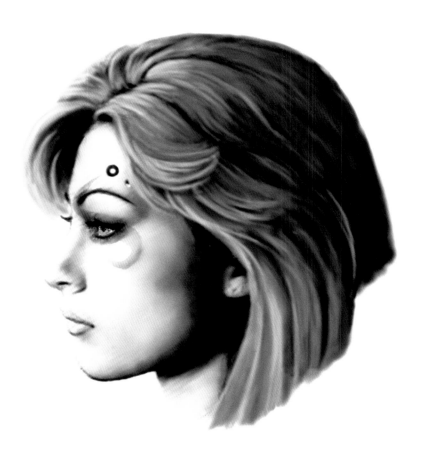

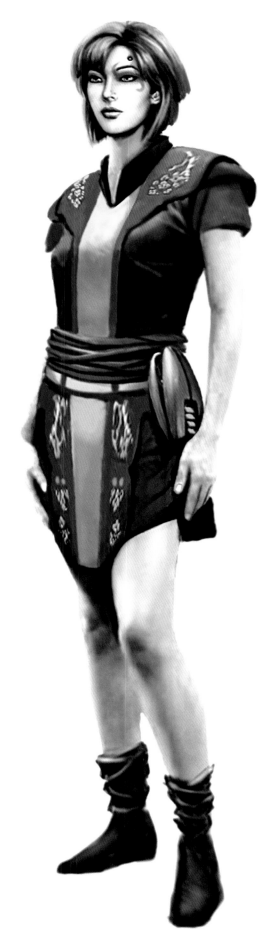

ENDORA

Left: Digital, private work

LORIEN (character from *Endora*)

Above and right: Digital, private work

As an experiment I made some colour comic pages in my hyper-realistic style. The starting point was: 'what would happen if gods existed but were completely crazy?' The story is set on another planet, Endora, where civilization and scientific progress were at the peak of their splendour. But a virus, the Serx, able to arouse the primordial human instincts, escaped from control and spread over the atmosphere, causing a global war that destroyed the civilization and killed most Endorian inhabitants. Terrorised by the virus and looking forward to finding a treatment, the last survivors took shelter on Daliah, an immense space station in orbit around the planet, which was now upset by the war and not able to support life any more.

In the following years an idea took hold on the space station: it was useless to keep on employing Daliah's resources on the planet, which by that time was considered irremediably infected. It would be better to concentrate on the development of Daliah. All contact with Endora stopped, and the planet became from that moment taboo for fear of the virus.

Many years pass, and no one from Daliah goes to Endora. In the meantime the population on Daliah increased, and the station was enlarged until it created an enormous ring around the planet.

The story begins about 1000 years after the Big War, when the virus Serx, after many centuries of quiescence, infects Elesia, Daliah's governor, who belongs to the order of the Organizers, the powerful controllers of the station. Elesia gets to know of some survivors living on the planet and some new civilizations are developing. The governor, who does not know she has been infected, sees the new inhabitants as a threat to Daliah's security. They must be destroyed …

ELESIA

(character from *Endora*)

Below: Digital, private work

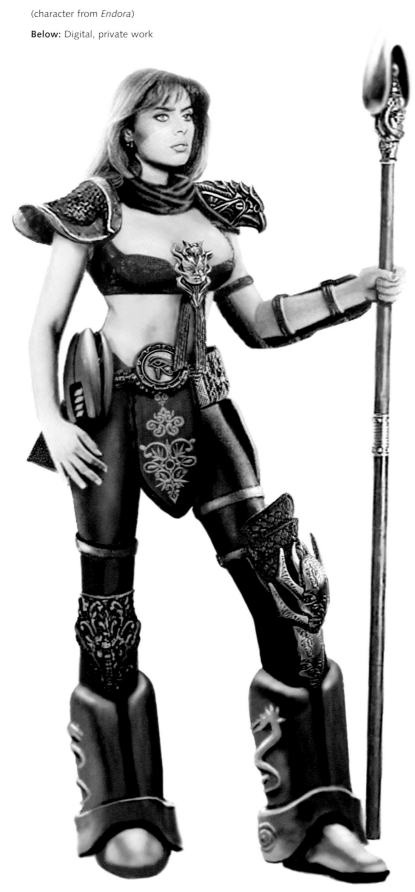

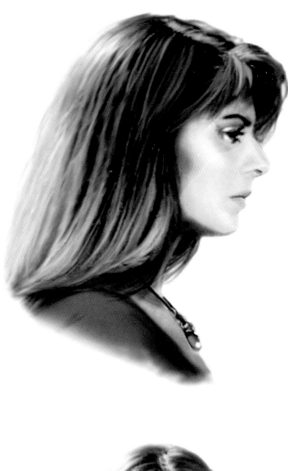

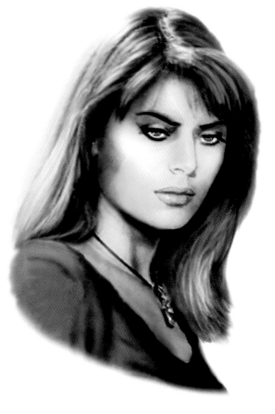

ENDORA page 2

Right: Digital, private work

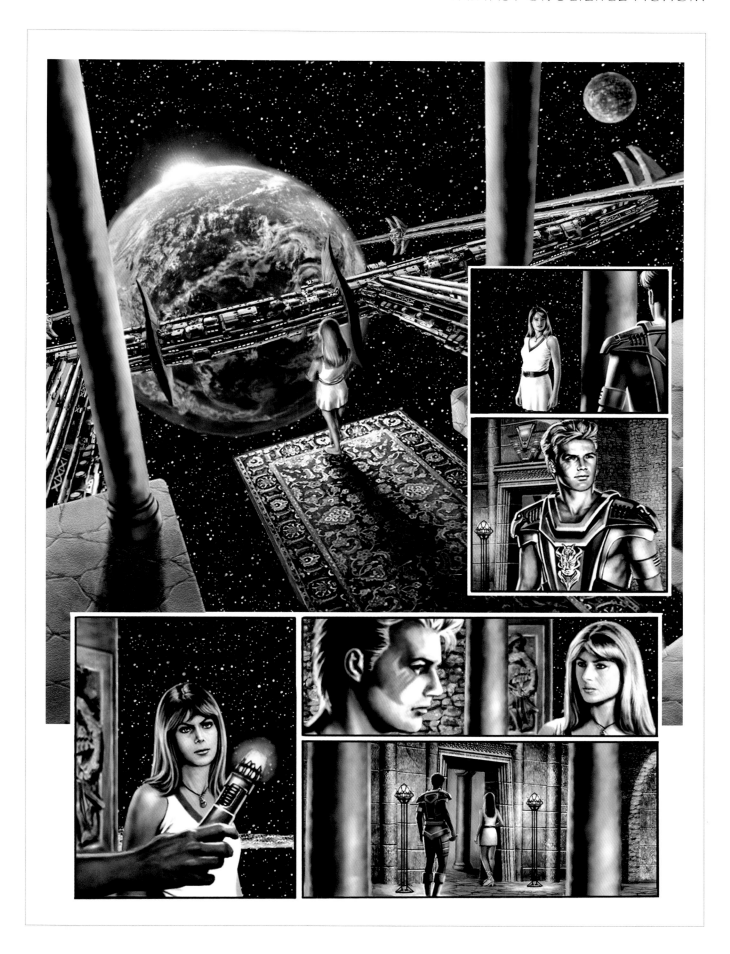

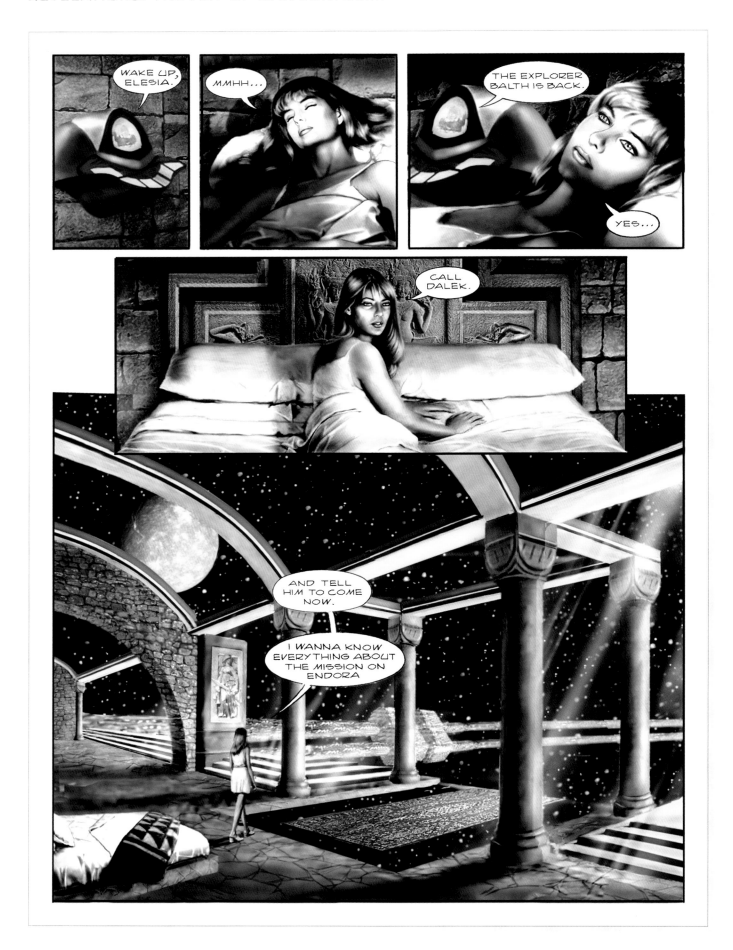

KALTHECK

(character from *Endora*)

This page: Digital, private work

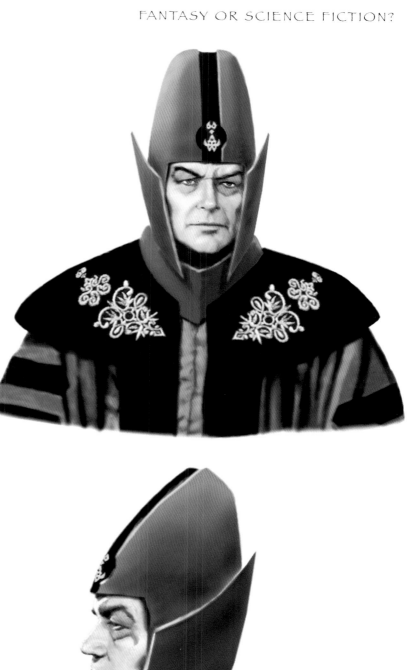

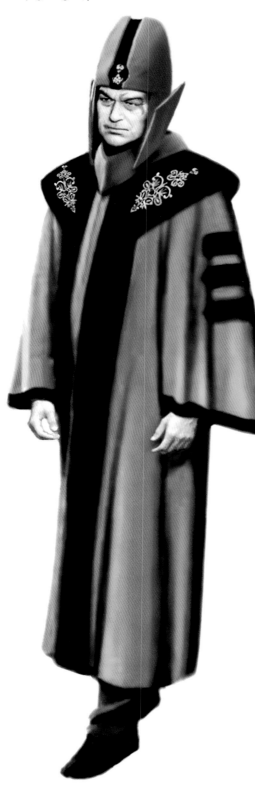

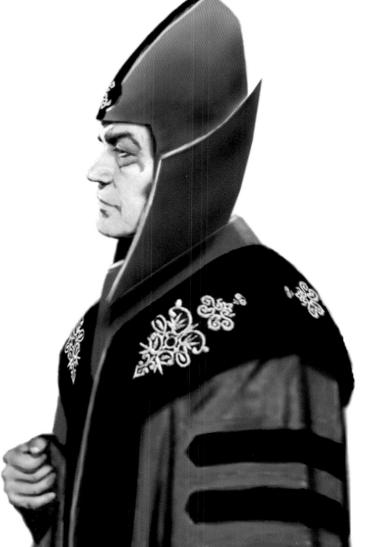

ENDORA page 3

Left: Digital, private work

Art and the Market

Being a good illustrator does not automatically mean you will find work easy to come by. You can be a genius, but if nobody recognizes it, your talent in itself won't lead to work. Making a profession out of your greatest passion is certainly quite difficult, but I'm convinced that if you have drive, if your living depends on your art, as an illustrator you will be able to give your best. This is the only way of establishing yourself. If you have no drive you become lazy and don't push yourself as far as you can. It seems masochistic to say so, but the major difficulties I have had in my life have matured me as a person and therefore as an artist. If you don't live your life intensely, you will never produce anything wholly original.

Forming contacts with publishing houses is almost an art in itself. In this respect the advent of the Internet has changed the way I present my portfolio, bringing the whole world into my home. This is certainly an advantage for someone as lazy as me, who looks on specialist trade fairs as a penance in which I participate against my will. People who regularly use the Internet for work are well aware of the advantages, but illustrators are particularly fortunate because of the opportunities it offers to visit the sites of publishers that interest them and then getting into contact via e-mail. If possible, I always try to get to know my clients personally because I believe in the personal relationship, but, since I began selling my work all over the world, this has become impossible. The Internet nullifies distance and time and is a superb channel of advertising because it makes my portfolio visible to anybody at any moment via my website. I can keep up to date with everything that publishing houses produce and follow the latest graphic trends so I do not fall behind in terms of new styles. Each month I automatically send a newsletter to everyone registered on my site. I can keep them updated about the latest developments in my work and receive valuable input from them. The newsletter is a form of mini-monthly psychotherapy for me – I can focus my thoughts and keep those who follow me in touch with the less visible aspects of my work. It is extraordinary how little those who don't work in the profession know of its details. When I explain that it takes at least two weeks to do an oil-based illustration, people are surprised. Similarly, when I say it takes four days with a computer, they always think it is a really long time, because 'the computer does it all' and 'it is not real art' because it wasn't produced on paper – as if the art is actually present in the tools, not in the mind of the artist.

The value you give to your own finished work is often not the same amount as you are paid for it, but this is also true the other way round: I often do pieces that I'm not satisfied with even if I'm well paid for them. So what is the real value of a piece of art? If by value we mean economic

OLYMPIC POLITICS

Right: Digital, inside illustration for *Fantastical Visions II*, Fantasist Enterprises

When the King of the Gods decides it is time for him to take back power, he discovers that the political climate has changed too much for his brand of thunderbolt-enforced leadership. I really enjoyed drawing Zeus as a shaven and smartly dressed businessman, but still bearing his lightning bolts.

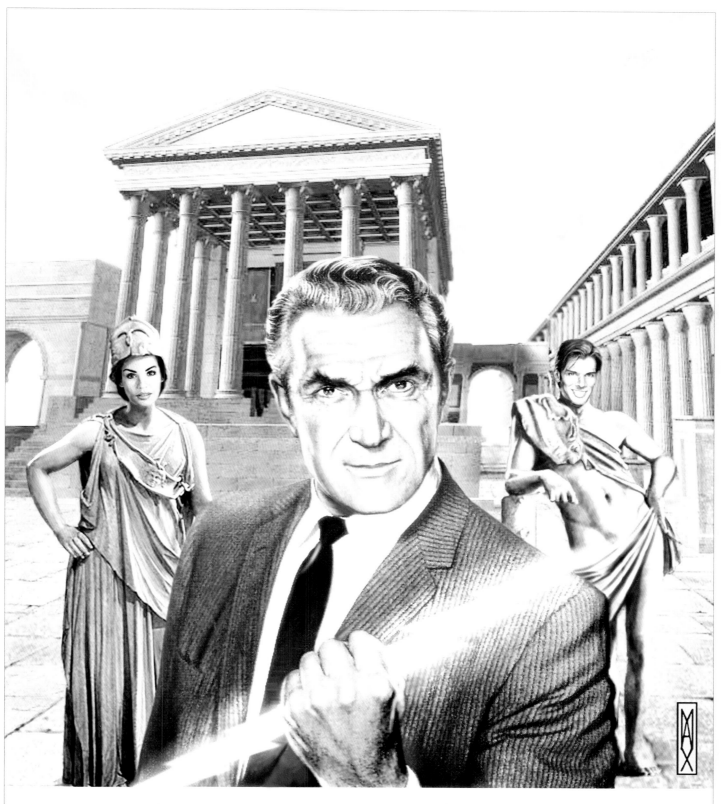

VOTE ZEUS

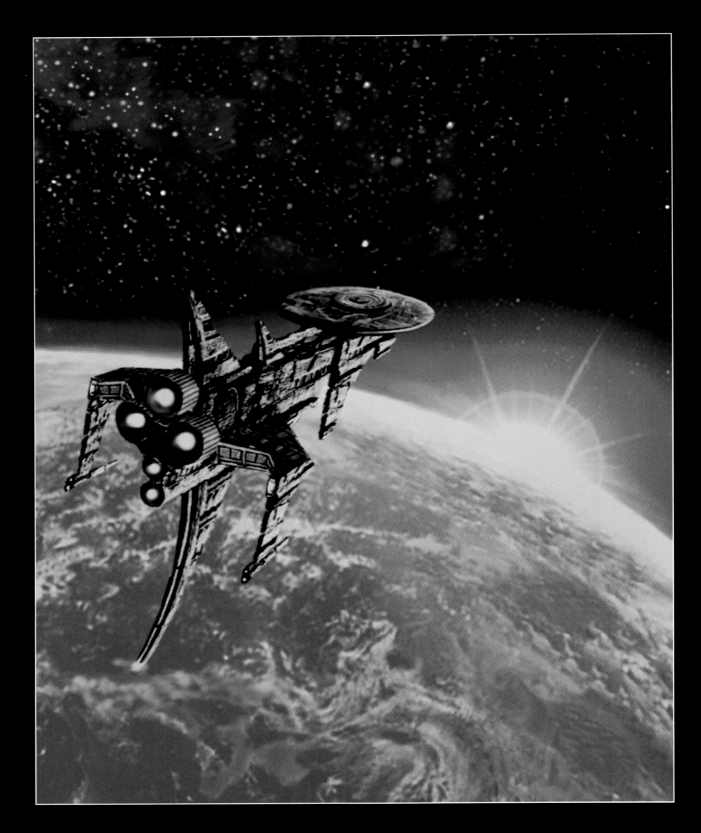

STAR BLADE

Above: Digital, Private work

The song of the stars calling us to our destiny. A simple image built with primary colours inspired by the immensity of the universe and all the mysteries and infinite adventures waiting for us.

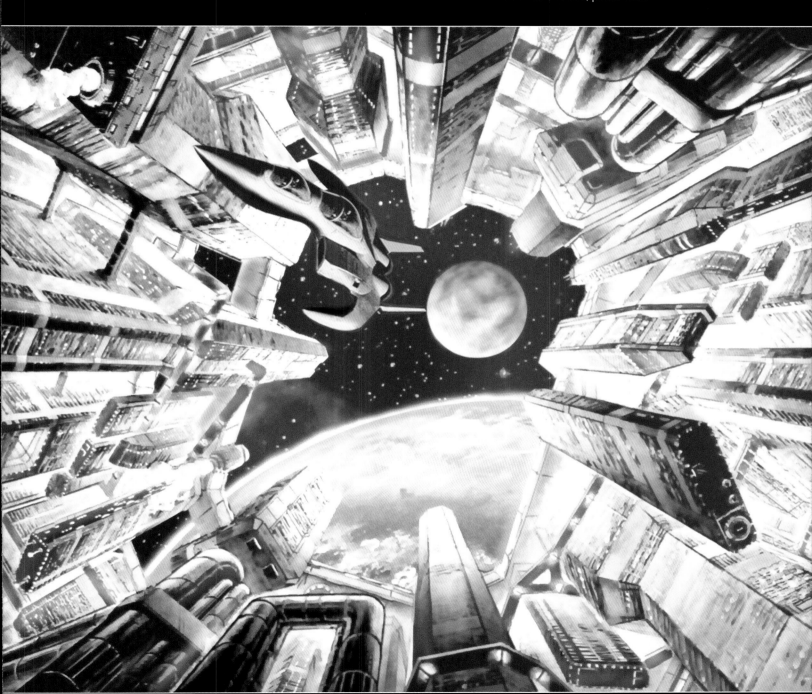

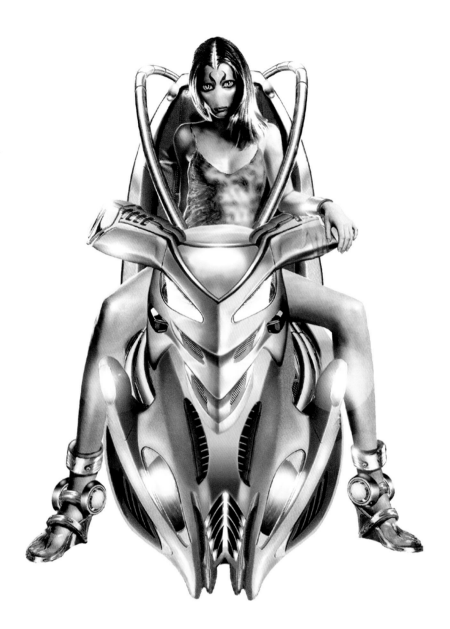

NEW BEGINNING

Right: Digital, private work

The spaceships are leaving to discover new planets. When I started I wanted to create an image full of hope and trust in the enterprise of the human race of the future. I based the city in the background on the architecture of Venice and Istanbul.

TESMETH

Left: Digital, cover for the comics fanzine *Ink*

I like the absolute sense of an alien world that this work expresses. She really looks as if she has come from another dimension.

value, it depends on the market – in other words the maximum a customer is willing to pay for it. But this is not its absolute value – much depends on current trends. Many famous artists were re-evaluated many years after their death, while others were lauded during their lives and forgotten within a few years after their deaths. Perhaps the real value lies in the judgement of the critics. However, even the experts are not always to be trusted. I once presented an art director of a large publishing house with a piece I had done by computer. To show me that he knew how to find errors in a piece of work, he began to enlarge the image until a particular detail took up the entire screen, before being able to declare triumphantly: 'There! See there is a bit of smudging there?'

Essentially, the true value of a good piece of work is not determined by a price or opinion but rather by the intrinsic quality of the work itself, in the emotions it transmits to people when they look at it, in the way it recalls the beauty in the world, and in the way that humans are able to become almost eternal through the creation of something unique and unrepeatable.

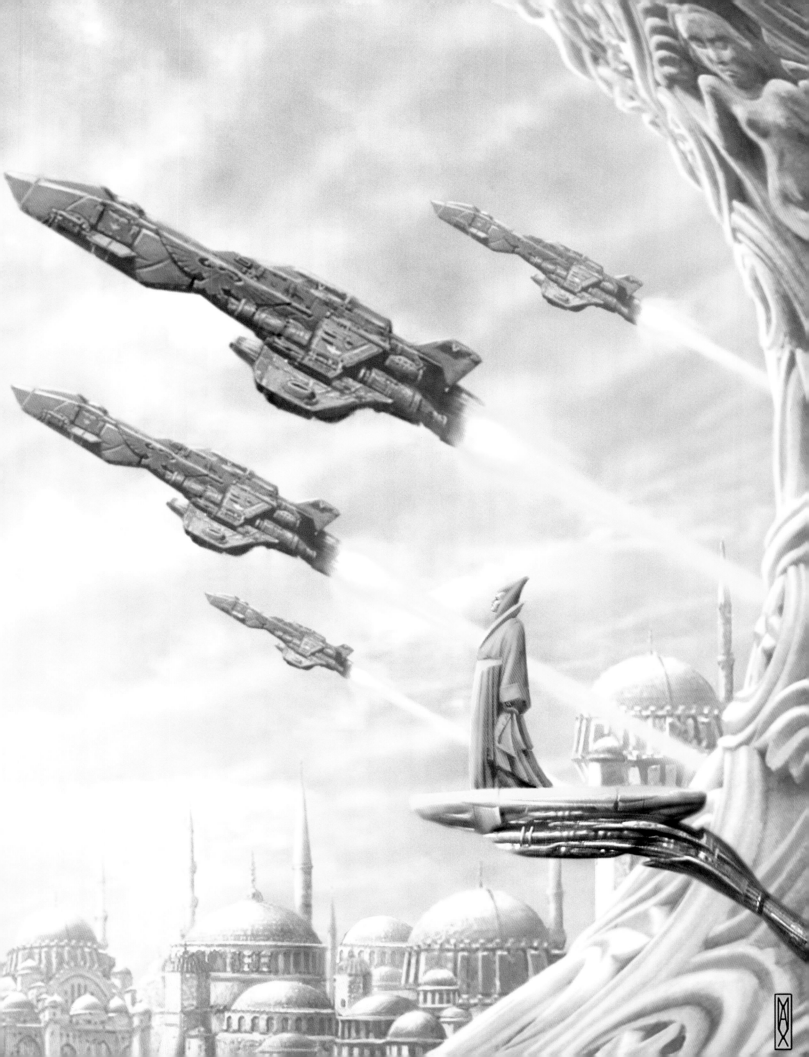

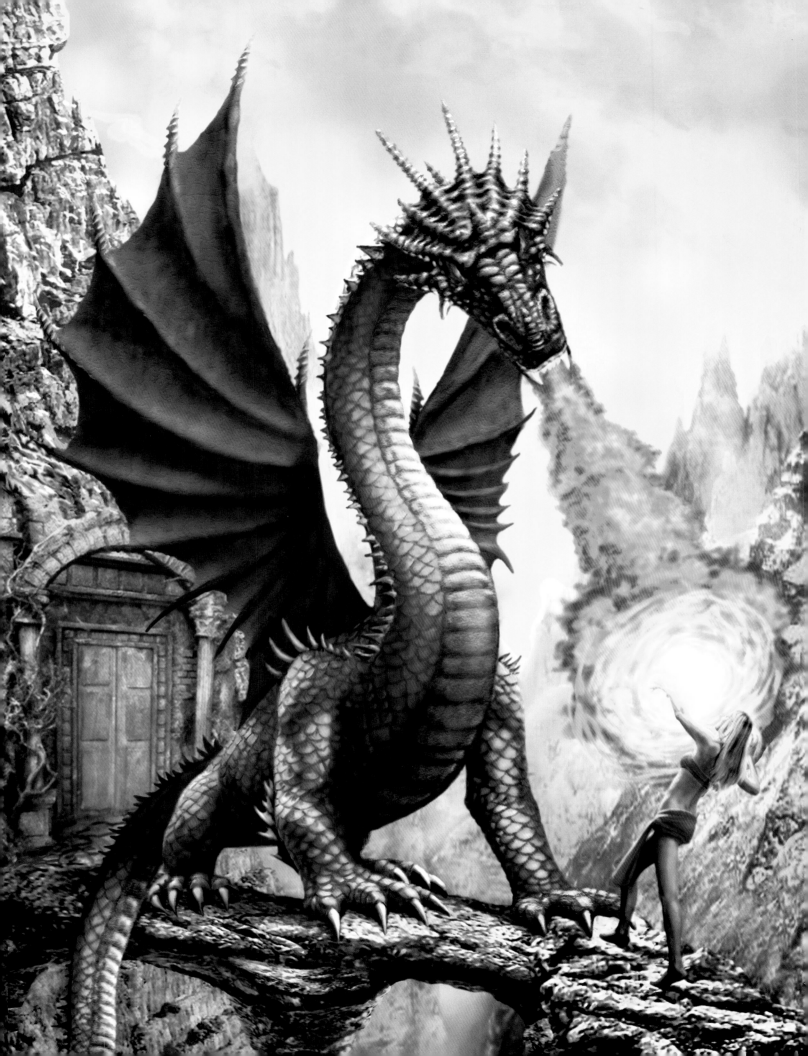

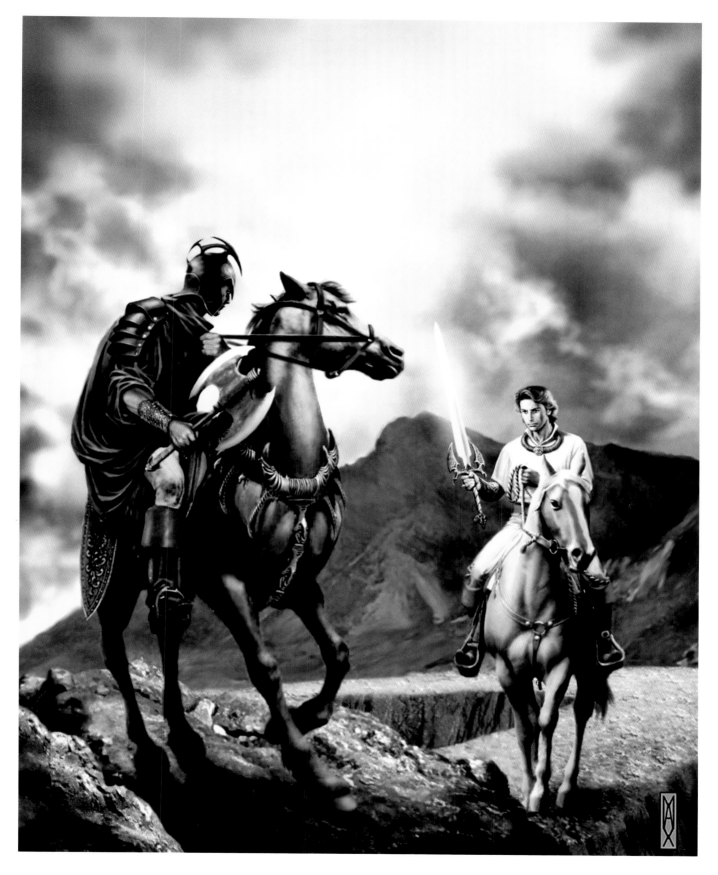

RED GUARDIAN

Left: Digital, private work

THE CONQUER OF THE THRONE

Above: Digital, hard cover for Robin Hobbs's *Des Königs Meuchelmörder*, Weltbild

PIN-UPS AND EROTIC ART

ntil now I have, on the whole, occupied myself with pin-ups, only occasionally touching on true erotic art. Interest in drawing the female form was a natural progression for me. Until a few years ago I was mainly interested in the dynamism of male bodies in motion and I loved drawing action and combat scenes. I then began to reflect on the balance of the features in a painting and to consider the female form as new territory to explore. I realized that male anatomy is easier to draw because the muscles are better defined and more evident, while women, having more delicate curves, require greater attention to find the correct contours.

Drawing the nude female is a test that very few artists are able to avoid. It is much more than a question of visual eroticism; it is the search for the essence of the female soul. The pleasure I get from drawing women is transmitted directly to the viewer, but what I love most about the female form is the balance, the grace of the pose, the expressiveness of the face – all those things that go beyond simple anatomical exhibition. A nude

BEAUTY AND THE BEAST

Right: Digital, cover for AST Publisher

The story of Beauty and the Beast appears in many cultures in different forms. Although the Beast takes on many guises (serpent, wolf, wild boar and this time dragon), he is never appealing in appearance even though he is rich and powerful. In this world of magic and wonder the true love of a beautiful girl will dispel the torment of the feral but gentle-hearted beast. I enjoyed using strong colours for this illustration.

THE LADY AND THE WARRIOR (detail)

Below: Digital, cover for *La dama e il guerriero*, *I Rosa*, Arnoldo Mondadori Editore

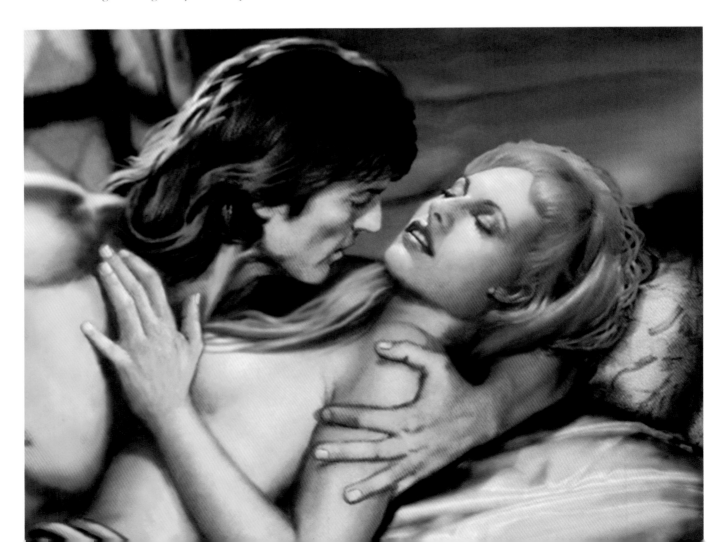

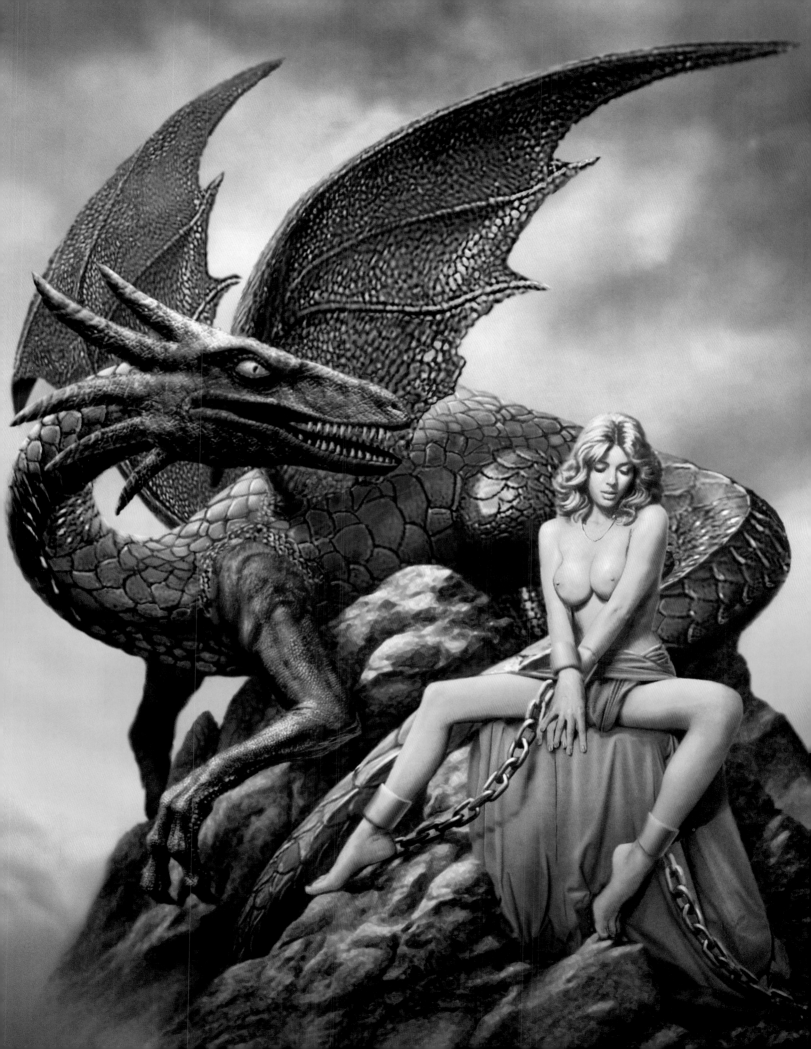

should be a springboard for discovering the meaning of femininity. A good female nude can delve into the mind of the model, reaching places that even she is unable to see, or capture the viewer with a look in a subtle game of seduction. More simply, it can be the study of a series of curves in harmony with each other. This is the case with *Babylon Slave* (see page 104) where the undulating body of the woman is emphasized by the roundness of the sofa on which she lies. In *Leda* (see page 105), however, I searched for a graphic solution, combining a nude in classic pose with a decoration I had seen on a wardrobe from the chambers of Napoleon III in the Louvre. I had certain works by Klimt in mind, such as *The Kiss* or *Danae*, a picture in which I love the expression on the face and the harmony of the curves. I have a very traditional approach to drawing, however, which, until now, has always consisted in representing reality as I see it. I therefore have a certain difficulty in reducing a body to a few brush strokes or filling the background with a series of patterns, as the Austrian master did. The final result of *Leda* is balanced in terms of composition and colours, but is not exactly what I had in mind. Comparison with the masters of the past is always a difficult activity. I always feel inadequate when I compare myself with them, and I am convinced that I am not good enough to try and reproduce what I see. But this is normal. I don't feel particularly gifted as an artist because for me it is a natural thing, just as breathing or walking is for others.

I am currently studying Synthetism. I would like to be able to transmit an emotion through a few simple graphics rather than representing everything three-dimensionally. This is particularly easy in erotic art because it is not always necessary to present an environment – it is sufficient just to create an atmosphere. *Seduction* (see page 114) is another attempt to use a simple aesthetic solution as a background. The oval that frames the two women defines the composition of the image, and the curve of the stone arch recalls the idea of circularity. The Sapphic love represented in this illustration is a frequent theme in this form of art, but even here I try to represent meanings that go beyond sex between women. The vaguely animalistic gestures and the darker skin of one of the women represent Evil; the other woman with pale skin, seduced by her embrace, is Good, unable to resist the other.

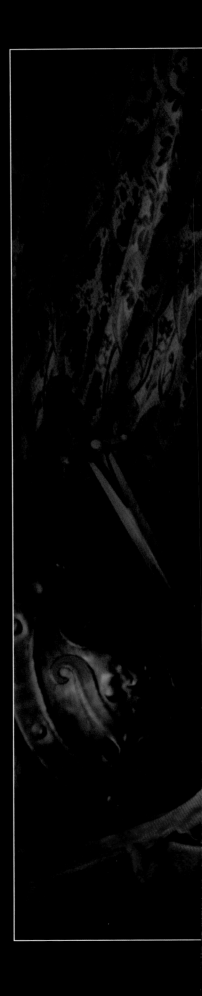

LADY AND DRAGON

Right: Digital, private work.
I like her long-limbed and well-endowed body and the special twinkle in her eyes. I search for the magic touch in my pictures, improving on nature by making the heads smaller and the legs and torsos longer. She looks real, but you can't touch her …

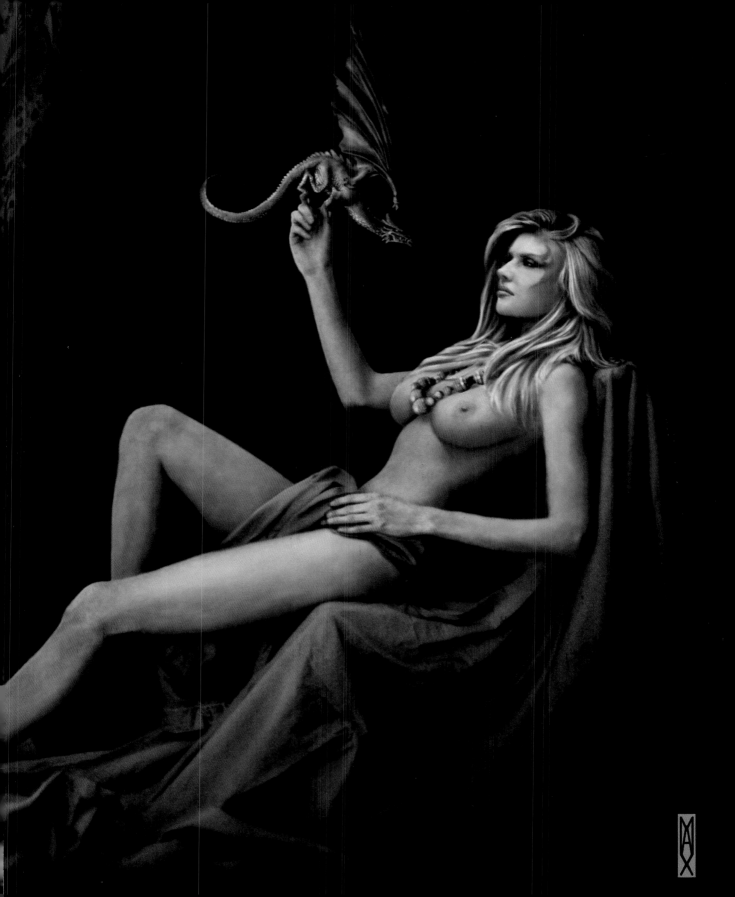

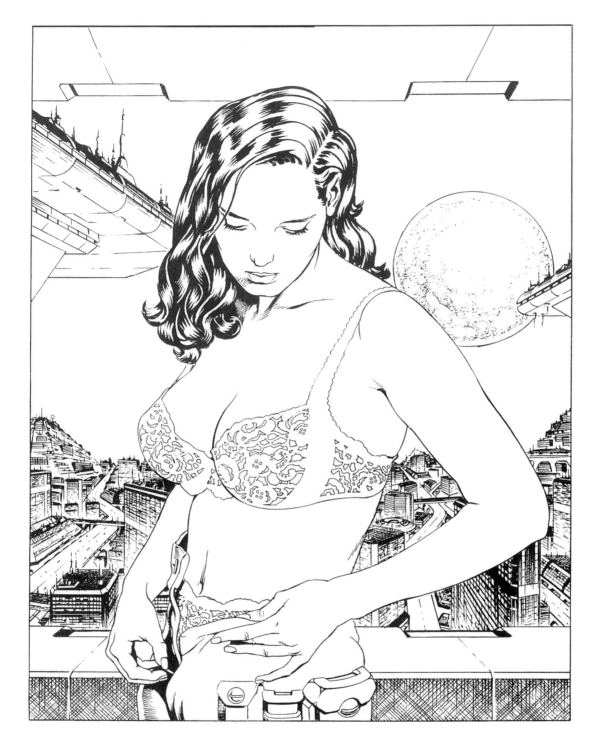

LUTHIEN

Right: Digital, private work

The light filtering through the branches and falling on the skin was the most complex thing to represent. The woman has an overflowing sensuality, a feature that is not common in my work, but it has been an amusing exception to the rule.

Erotica can be at times, merely a means of suggesting something else. In *May* the girl is undoing her trousers, creating great expectancy in the viewer. There is no vulgarity, but great naturalness in the gesture. I find that too much erotic art is simply in bad taste – I love drawing women who are elegant in their pose and seductive in their intentions, without ever showing explicitly sexual poses. It is more intriguing to suggest than to show, and a partially clothed woman is always more erotic that a totally naked one.

I'd also like women to find my pin-ups interesting, and so I try to accentuate the elegance of the composition and explore the psychology of

MAY (was ELENA)

Above: Ink on paper, 8.5 x 11.5 inches Pin-up for Sergio Bonelli Editore

I had to draw May, a character from the comic book *Nathan Never*. It would have been printed on high quality paper and given as a gift to the readers at the stand of Bonelli Comics at the comic's fair of Milan. I did it, but the publisher said it was too sexy for the young readers and didn't use it…

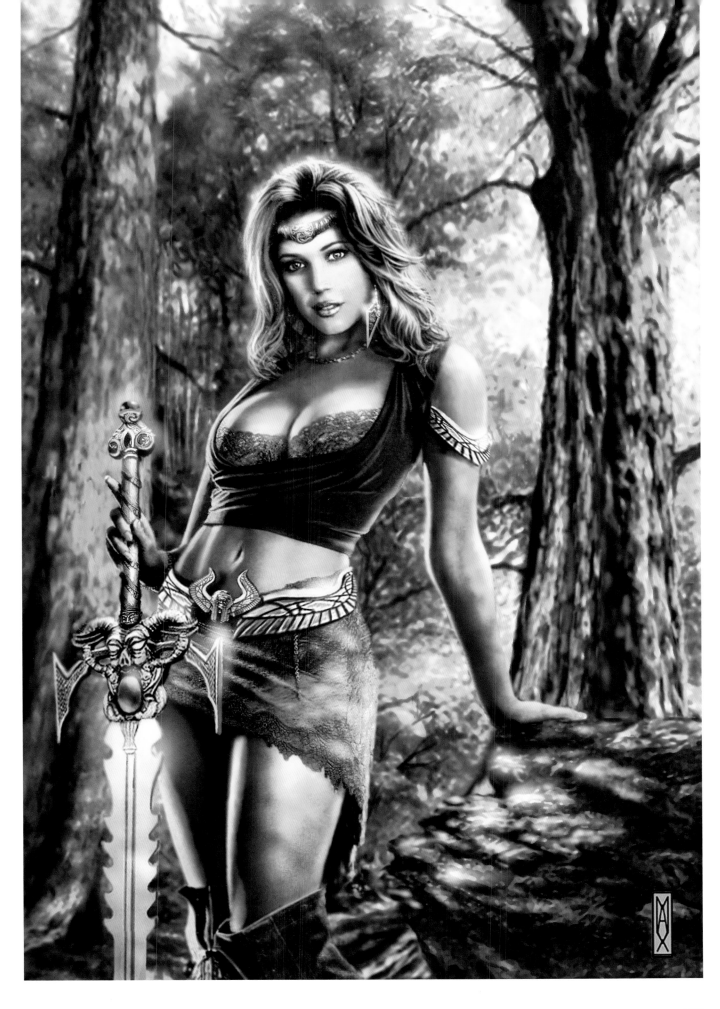

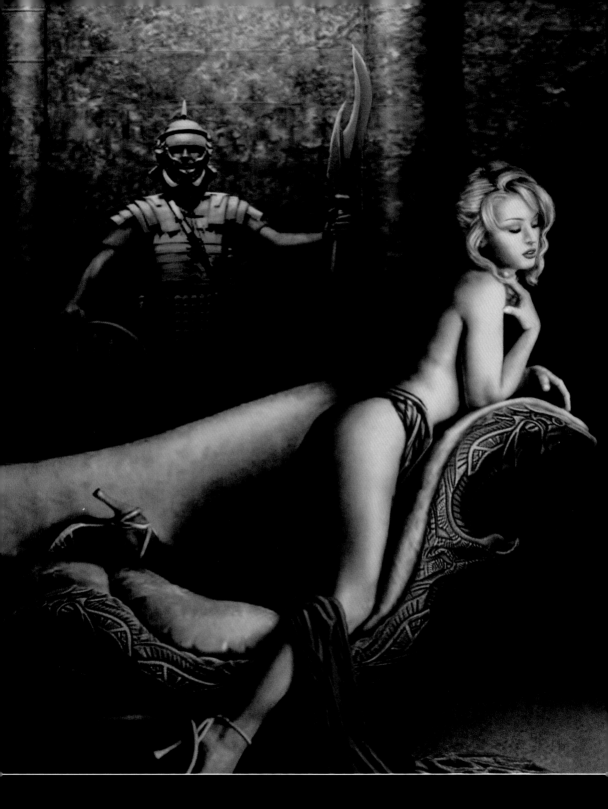

BABYLON SLAVE

Above: Digital, private work

As I was drawing I was imagining an ancient palace in the Arabian Desert, where this Babylon Princess is kept in captivity, waiting for the commander of the invading army

LEDA

Right: Digital, private work

Again, I'm trying to give a new meaning to the word 'womanliness'. I think I was also somehow inspired by the ancient greek statues for this piece

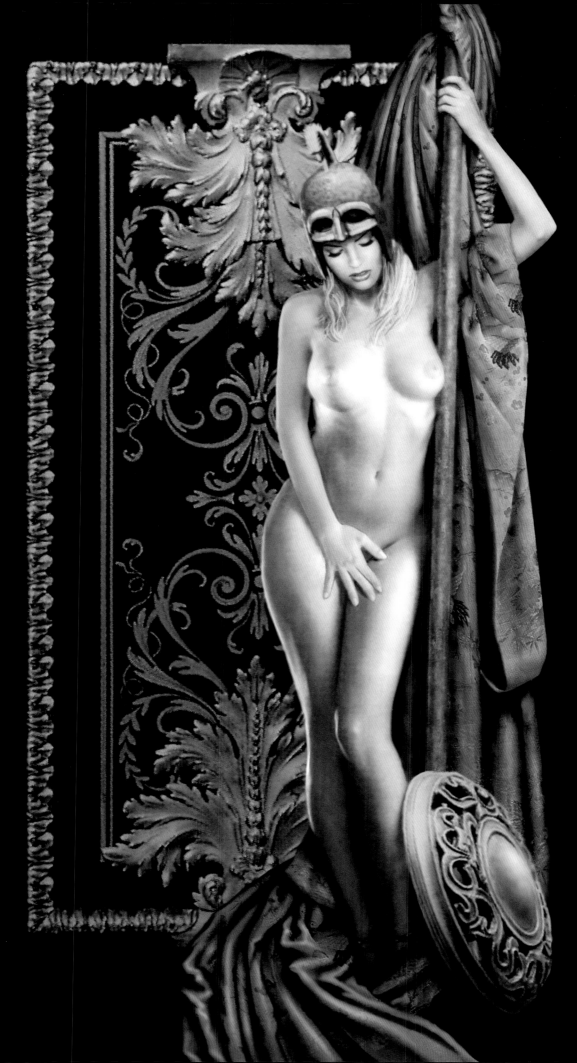

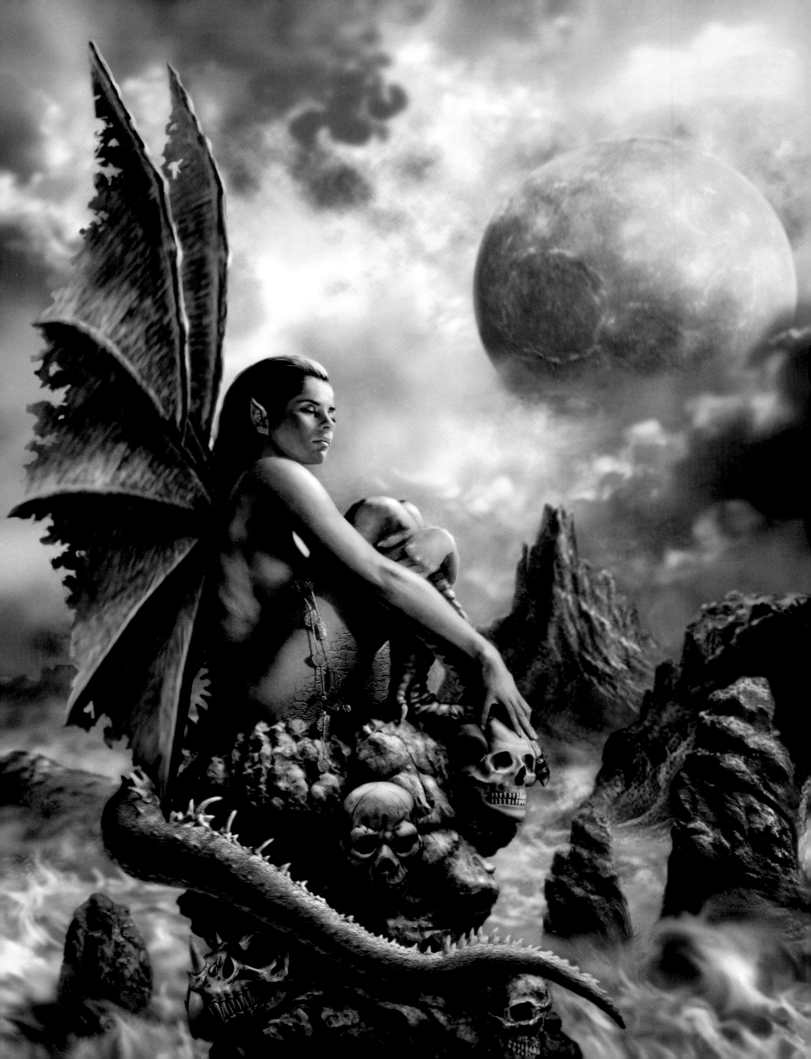

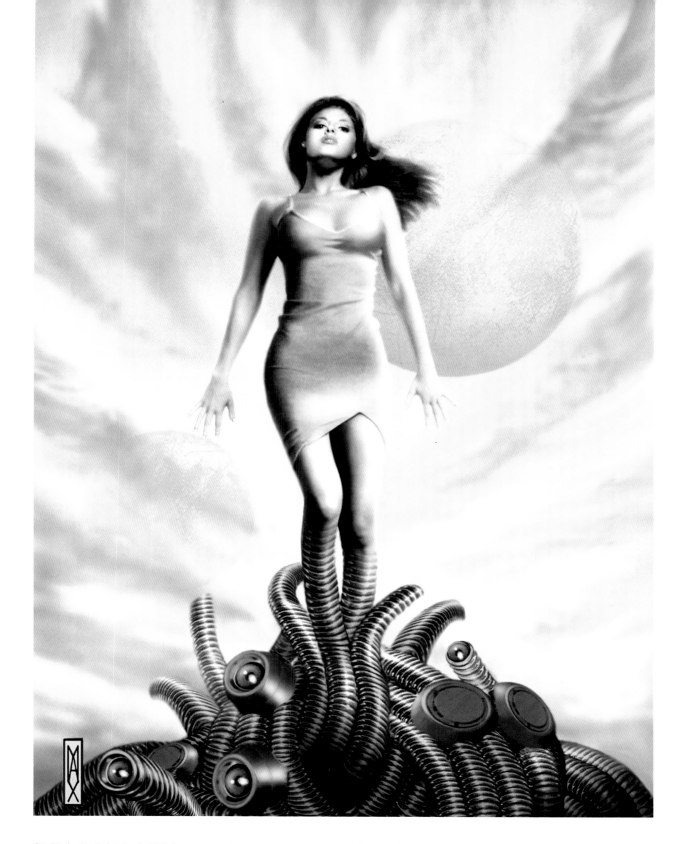

DRAGON LADY

Left: Digital, private work

In Chinese culture the Dragon Lady is a woman who is seductive and desirable but at the same time untrustworthy. She has the power to hypnotize her male rivals, seducing them and using them for her own desires. The skulls lying on the rocks are a warning to those who dare to approach her.

FREEDOM

Above: Digital, cover for Eura Editoriale

This can almost be considered the sequel to *Cyberangel*, when the woman finally frees herself from the chains oppressing her. But is it real freedom? In fact, her legs are still bonded to the structure beneath her. Looking at it now, I realize I was unconsciously inspired by a painting that was hung in my home when I was a child: a woman who rose from the roots that anchored her to the ground.

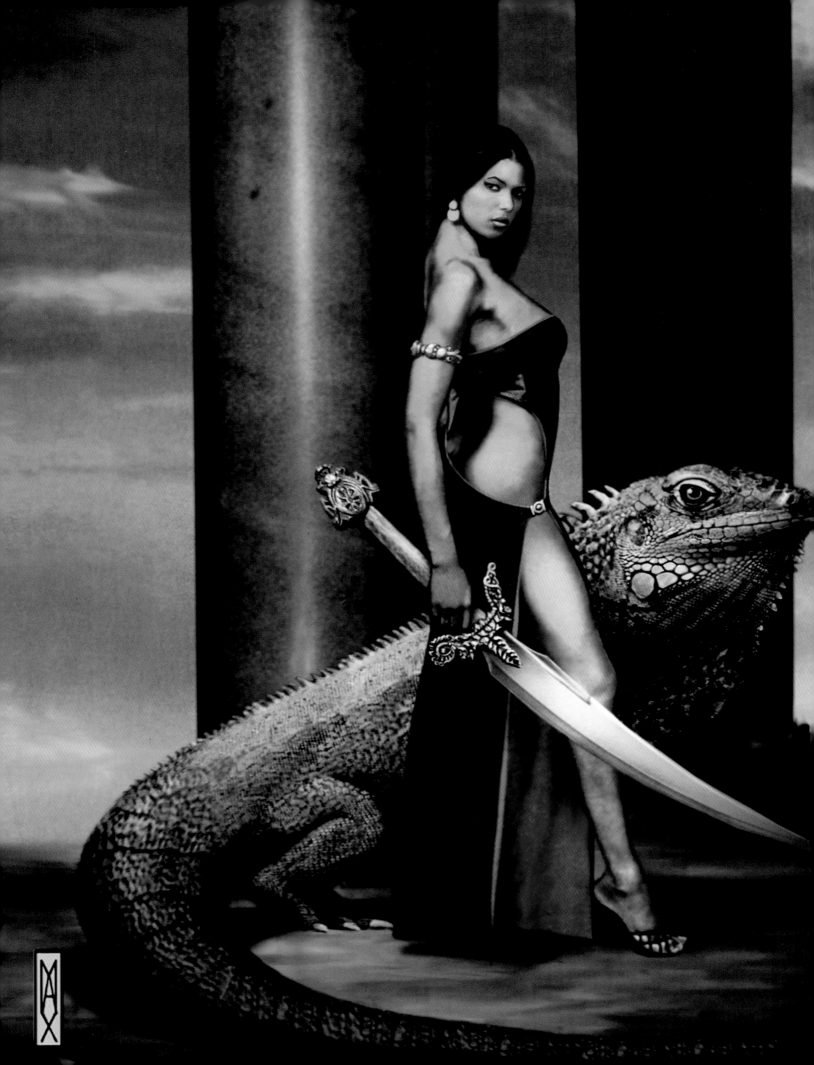

BLACK PRINCESS

Left: Digital, cover for *Eura Editoriale*

Balance and composition are the keys here. The observer's eye naturally ends up on the face of my princess. Elegance and refinement were the words that inspired me as I drew. I received some letters from people telling me how glad and astounded they were at the way I depicted this black beauty, because black art is quite hard to find.

THE MACKENZIES ~ ZACK

Right: Digital, cover for *Un Uomo Difficile*, *I Rosa*, Arnoldo Mondadori Editore

my models. For this reason, I was pleased to receive appreciation from women for *Black Princess*. They underlined the fact that they were finally seeing a true black woman, not just a black version of Pamela Anderson. I love giving my female characters their own personalities and each face its own particular features, because every face is the mirror of a different soul, and I do not want my art to reflect only physical appearance. I want to delve into the essence of my subjects, a goal that I do not yet feel I have fully achieved. I don't want to treat the women I represent as nothing more than objects, and I don't want to run the risk of making all women look the same, a habit that unfortunately characterizes the work of many erotic illustrators. Some people might say that accurately showing a woman's appearance is a way of revealing her character, but I think this is a limited approach, and I greatly admire painters such as Rockwell, who knew how to tell stories through the features of the faces he painted.

I used to illustrate the covers of romantic novels, a genre that has much in common with erotic art. You have to suggest passion in the image and

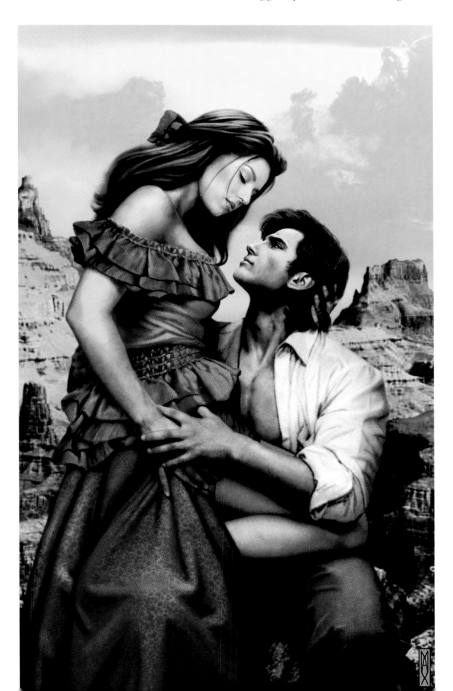

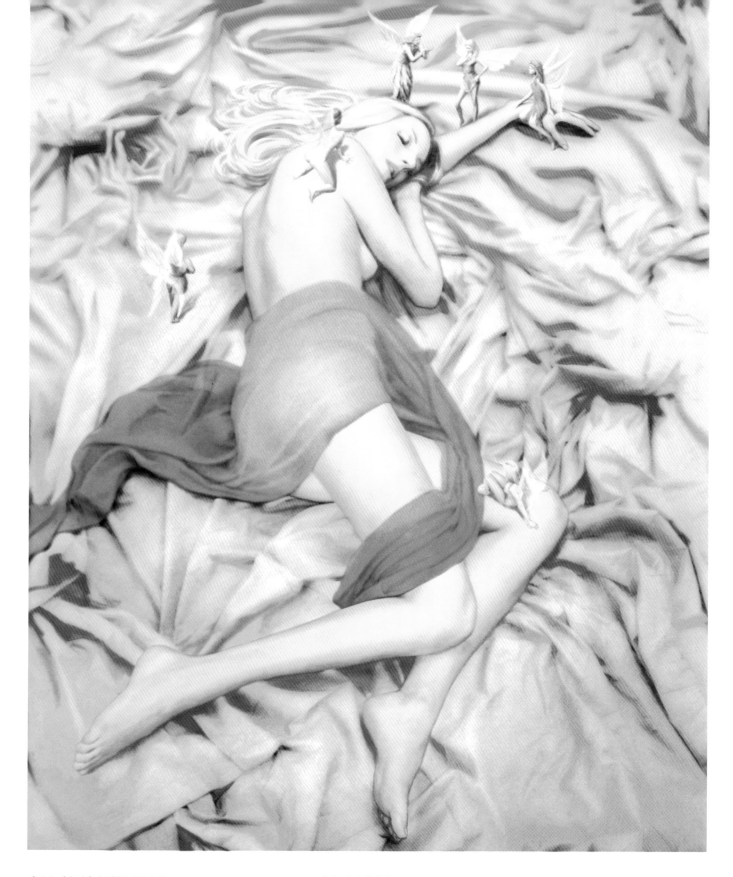

AN AWAKENING PROBLEM

Above: Digital, private work

A council of faeries discusses how to wake up this
sleeping beauty. I really love this piece, both for
the tender pastel colours and its subject.

ALANNA

Right: Digital, cover for *Lanciostory*, Eura Editoriale

I worked extensively on the face, which is unusual and not stereotypically beautiful.
While I was working, her oversized sword began to look more like a banner than a
weapon, and she now vaguely reminds me of a commander leading her troops to
victory, with the unusual light streaming in from the clouds, almost like a divine sign.

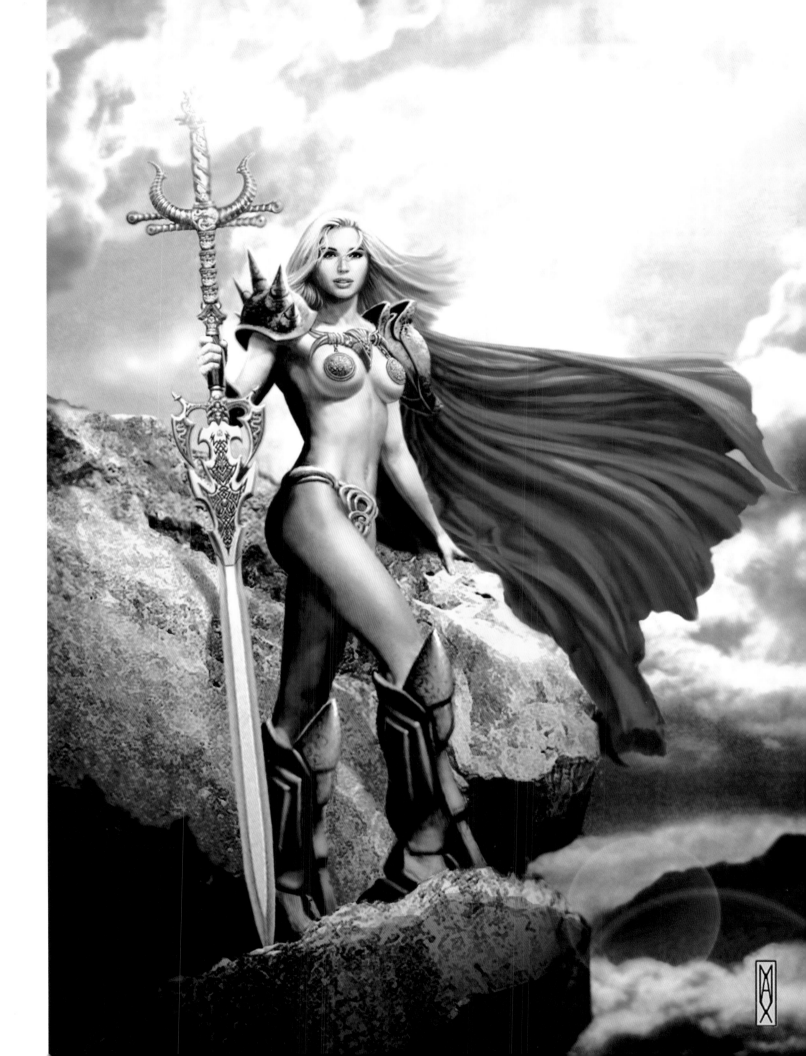

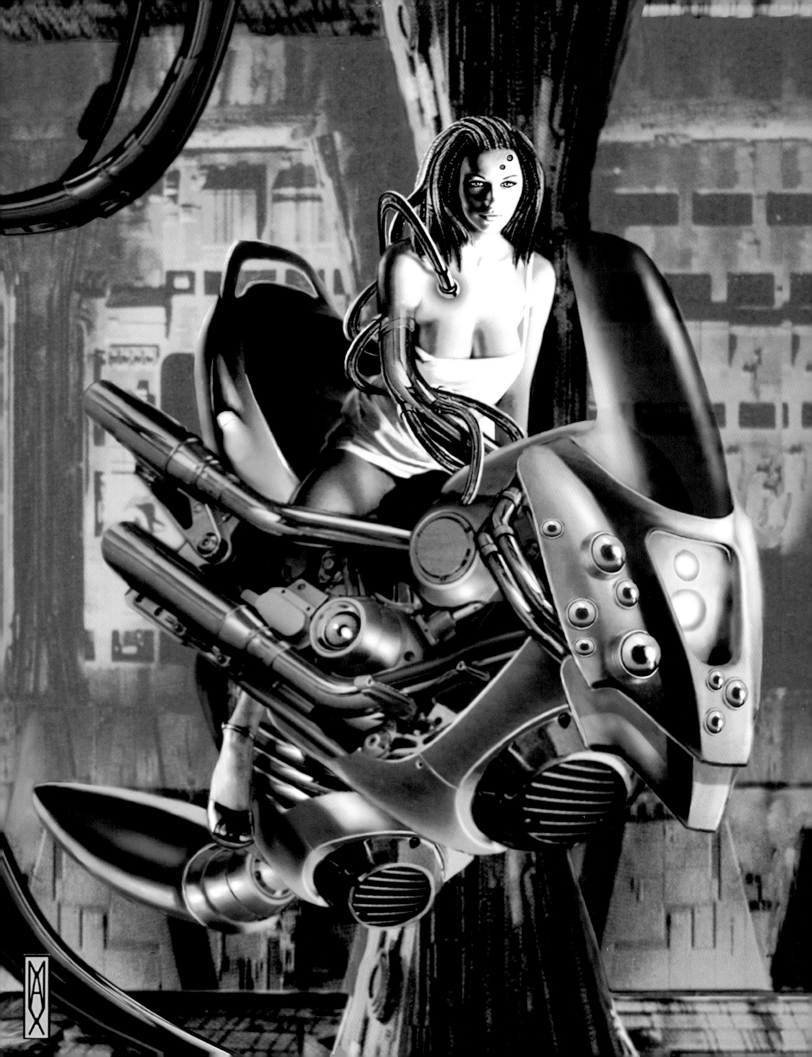

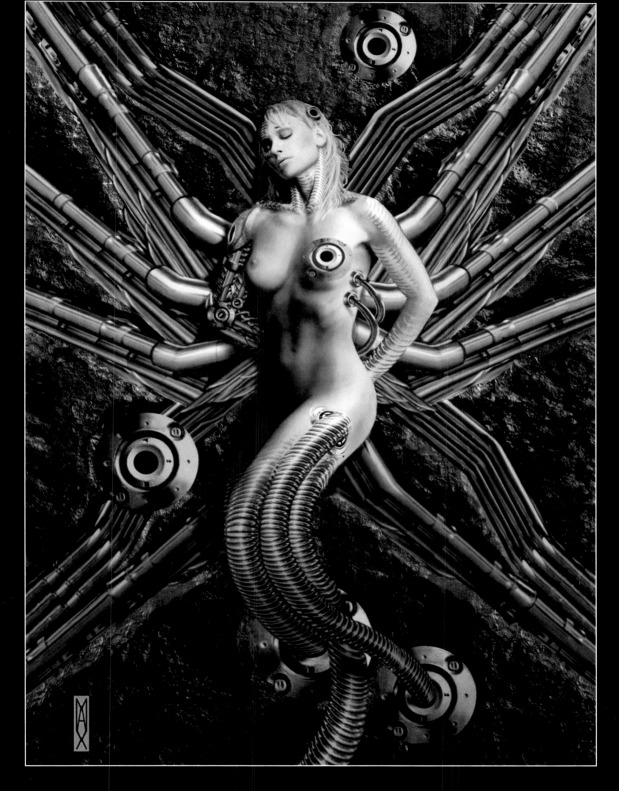

CYBERBIKER

Left: Digital, cover for *Lanciostory* Eura Editoriale

In a distant future, humans will have become one with their machines. There is no anguish in this illustration, yet the observer might feel rather alienated. I created the structure of the vehicle by remodeling one of the latest scooter models.

CYBERANGEL

Above: Digital, private work

Beauty violated and imprisoned by technology. I worked a lot on the tubes and face. I wanted to give her an unsettling, metallic look, so I used greenish-brown colours, with some shades of bloody red to create a sharp contrast. The pale skin, the half-closed eyes. The crucifixion.

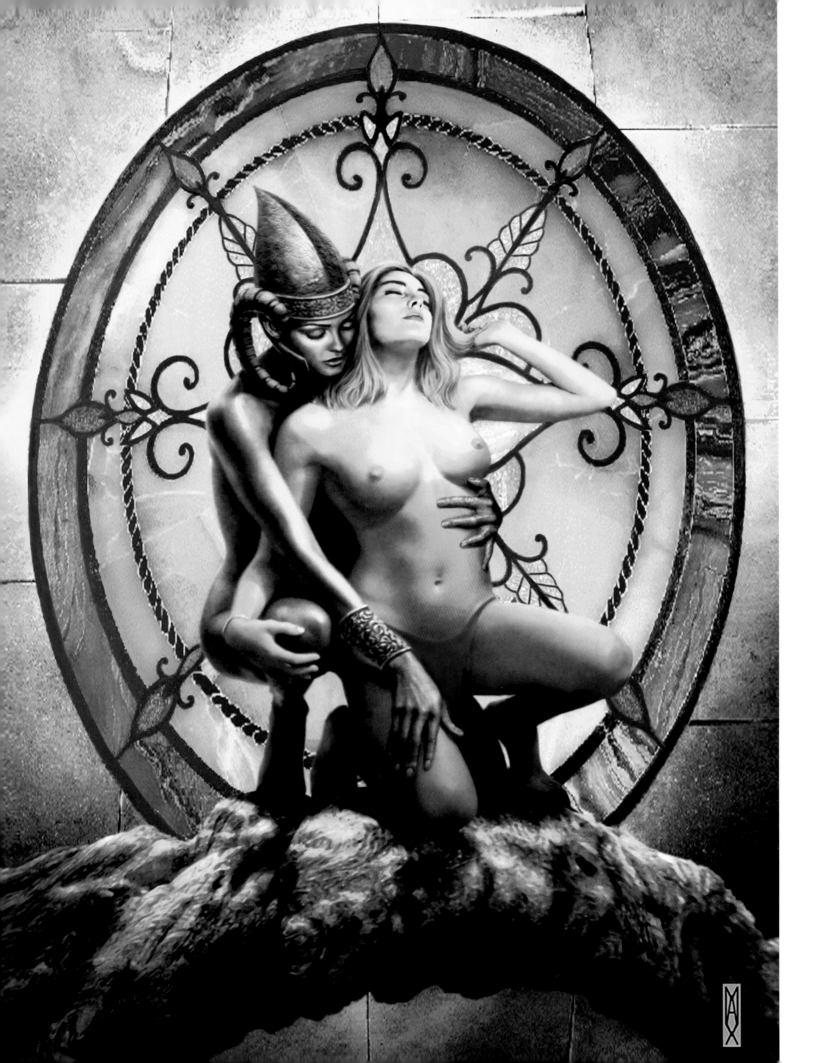

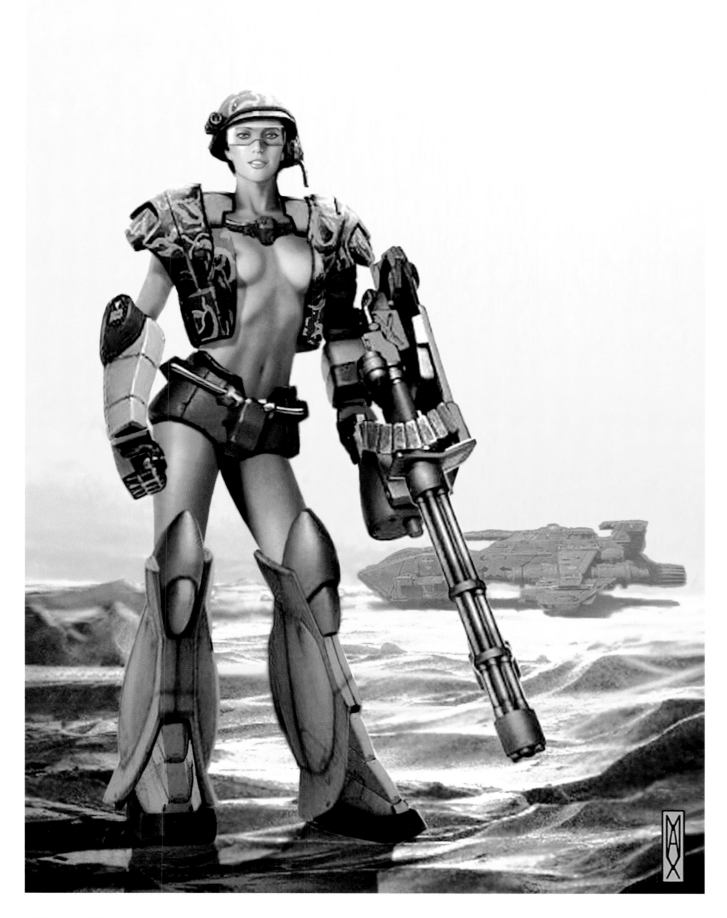

SEDUCTION

Left: Digital, private work

SPACE MARINE

Above: Digital, private work

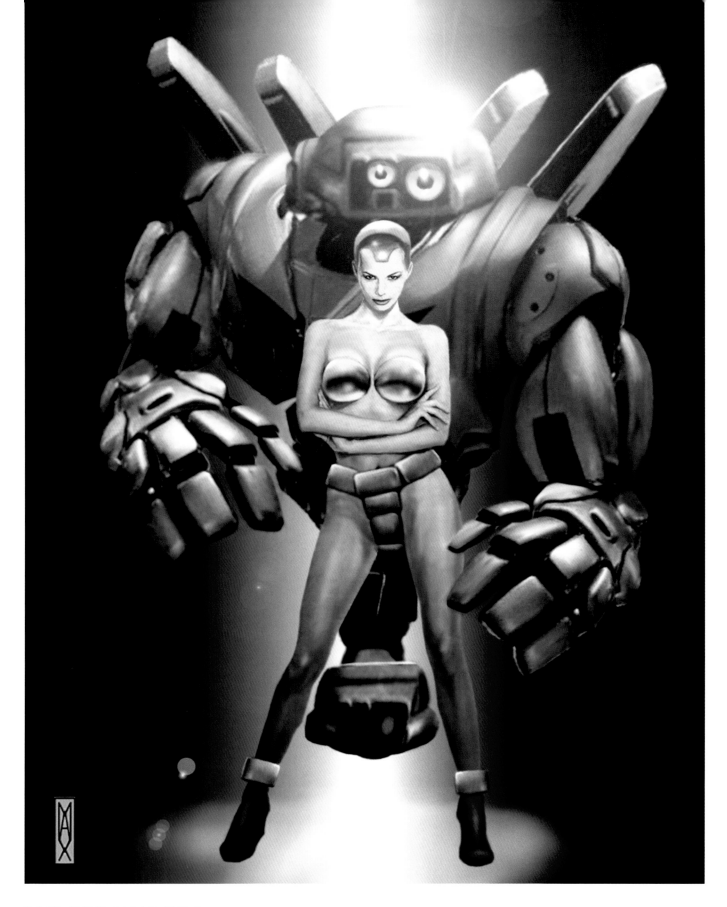

THE PERSUADERS

Above: Digital, private work

This is an extremely simple composition. I worked hard on the metallic rendering
of the robot and on the general mood. I love the girl's expression, too.

WILDERNESS

Right: Digital, unpublished

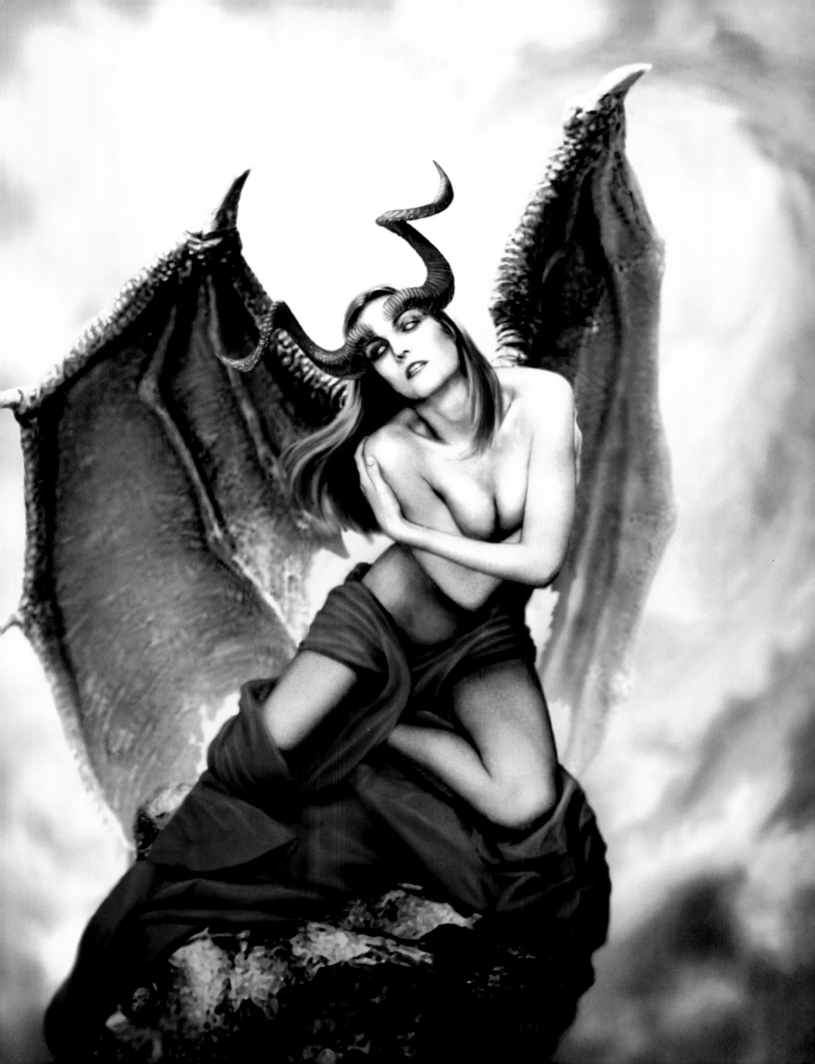

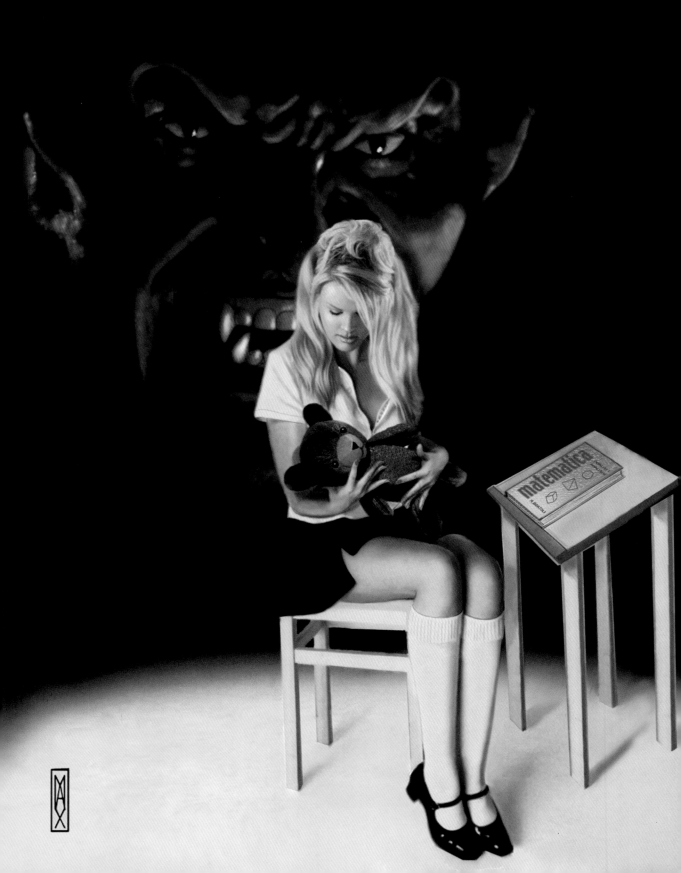

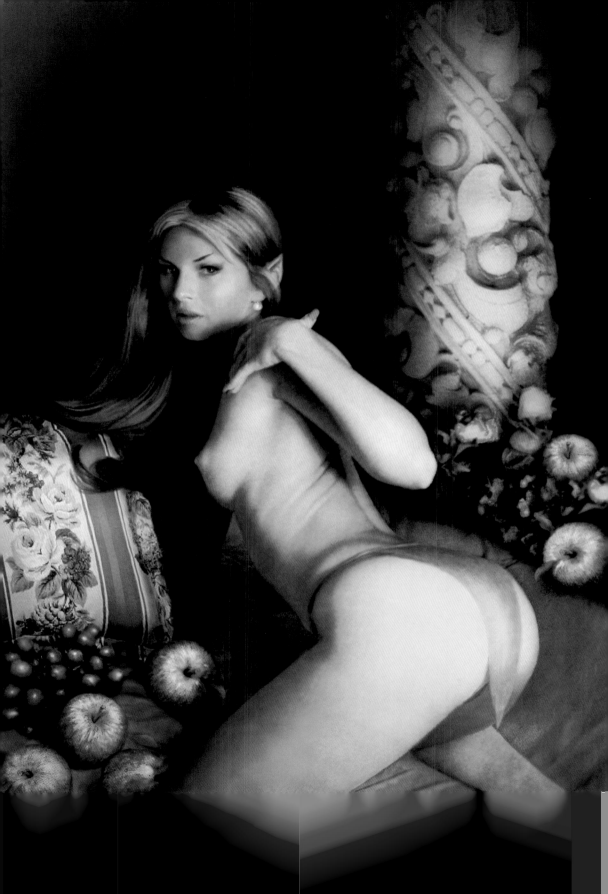

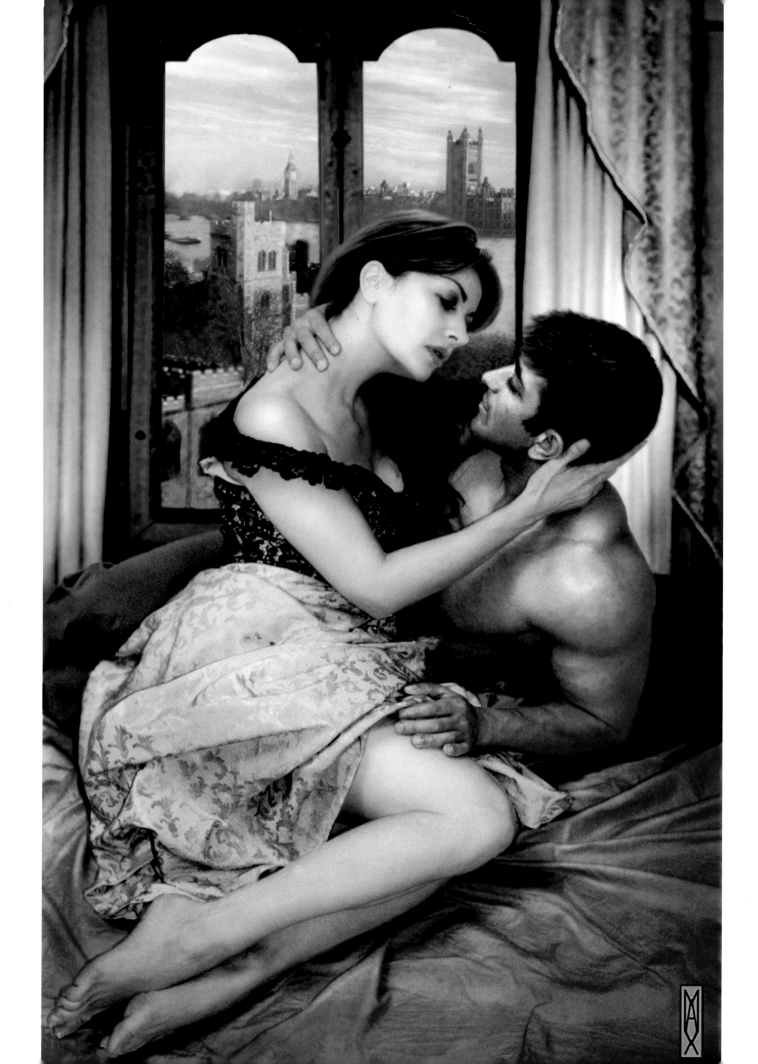

THE BRIDE MAKER

Left: Digital, cover for *Il fabbricatore di spose,
I Rosa,* Arnoldo Mondadori Editore

I like the delicate and subtle balance of reds and
greens on this cover. I used a light glow filter from
Photoshop to give a sheen to the character's skin.
The texture of the skirt was achieved by working on
that detail of the photograph.

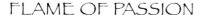

FLAME OF PASSION

Right: Digital, private work

I tried to give a feeling of overwhelming passion
through the skirt that swirls around the characters.
Somehow the colours reminds me of the old
romantic movies like *Gone with the Wind.*

Below: As you can see, I made many changes
between the preliminary photograph shown here
and the final picture. First of all, I added the flaming
background, then I enhanced the texture of the girl's
blouse and completely changed the face of the male
to make him show more passion – and, of course,
I added the hair to his head!

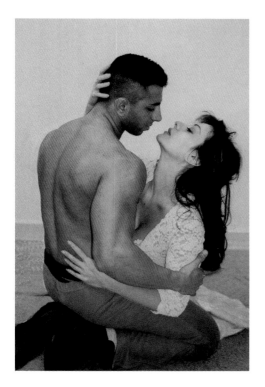

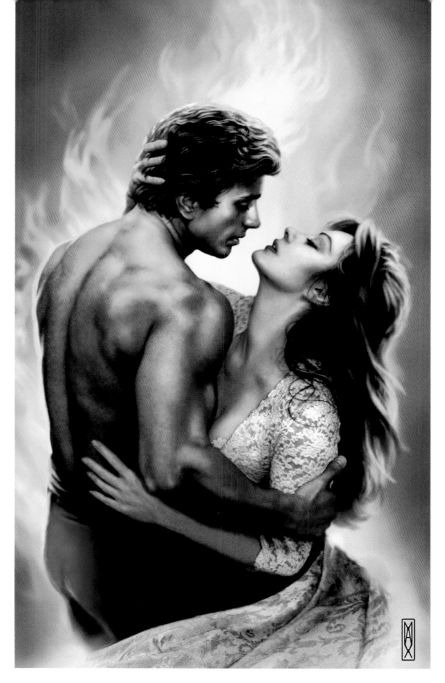

show as much as possible of both the man and the woman without
slipping into vulgarity, because the readers (generally women) want to
sense the passion without seeing explicit references to sex. The expressions
must be sensual, the men extremely masculine, the women beautiful and
seductive. The fire of passion that grips the protagonists is openly
represented by the illustration behind their backs in *Flame of Passion,*
whereas for other covers I chose more delicate situations, such as in *The
Bride Maker.* It was an enjoyable experience – I could analyse male
muscularity and portray fascinating women in a single image, without
worrying about the backgrounds, which were of secondary importance.
The most tedious aspect of this work is that the typical scene is always
the kiss on the neck, and it is difficult to continually come up with
different poses. One of the solutions to this particular problem is to
change the angle of the frame, another is to play around with the hang,
colour and styles of the clothes, which, in the case of period romances, are
always different anyway.

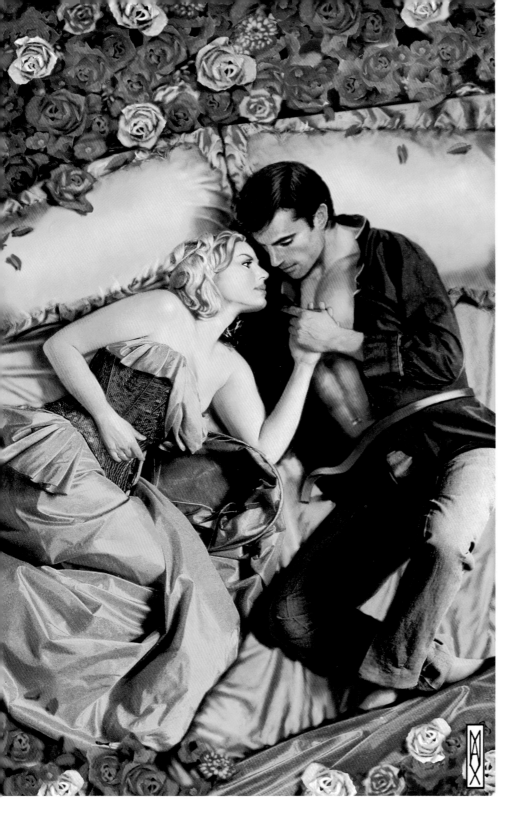

ONE THOUSAND HEARTS

Left: Digital, cover for *Millecuori, I Rosa*, Arnoldo Mondadori Editore
This is an unusual camera angle for a romance cover – it is as if the viewer is looking down from the ceiling. I didn't know what to use to surround the bed but I suddenly had the idea of a bed of roses.

SWEET WILD WIND

Right and below: Digital, cover for *Dolce vento selvaggio, I Rosa*, Arnoldo Mondadori Editore

The original photo had very weak colours, but I really liked the position of the models. I gave life to the final picture using strong reds and blues with yellow reflexes, as if they were completely plunged into the warm light of a summer's day.

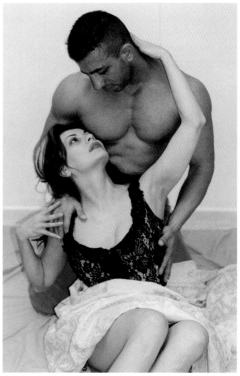

Artists go through various phases in their careers and evolve artistically by continually searching for new paths, without ever remaining still. It is difficult to say what the ultimate goal will be, even if it exists, but the journey each artist makes is important. I have learned that, in life, we often come across new and unknown paths, which lead us to things we could never have imagined and which are all the more fascinating for this very reason. It is like a long journey among the unknown planets of the universe. The number of pathways is infinite, but I have my art to explore them all.

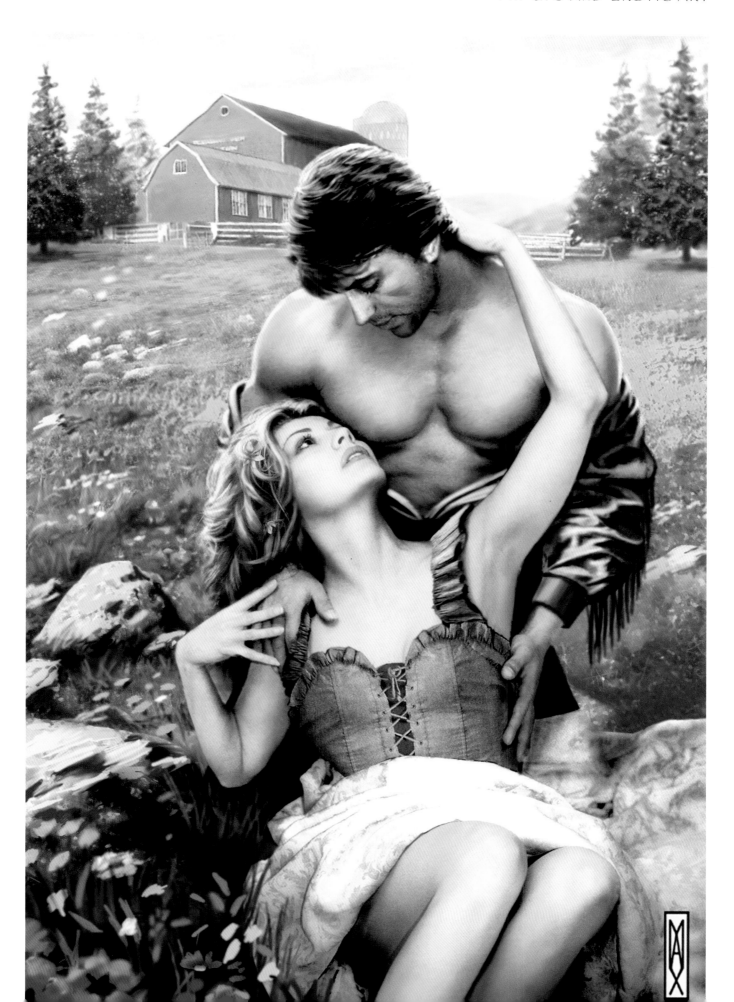

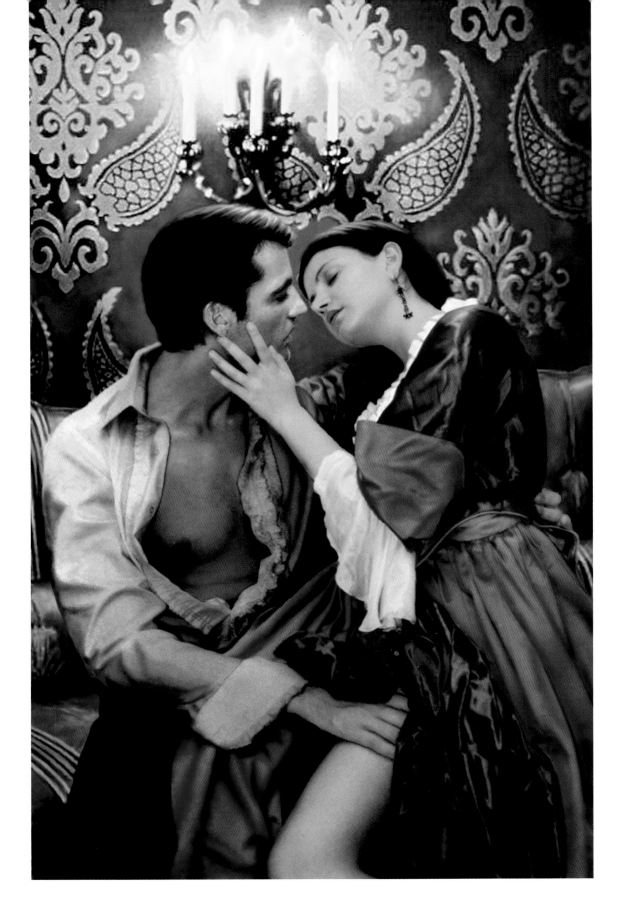

LOVE TIES

Above: Digital, cover for *Legami d'amore, I Rosa*, Arnoldo Mondadori Editore

THOUSAND YEARS EMPRESS

Right: Digital, cover for *Faeries*, Nestiveqnen Editions and Eura Editoriale

The mystery and magic of ancient oriental cultures are embodied in this timeless and charming empress. The 3D effect was achieved by using a real small miniature as a starting point.

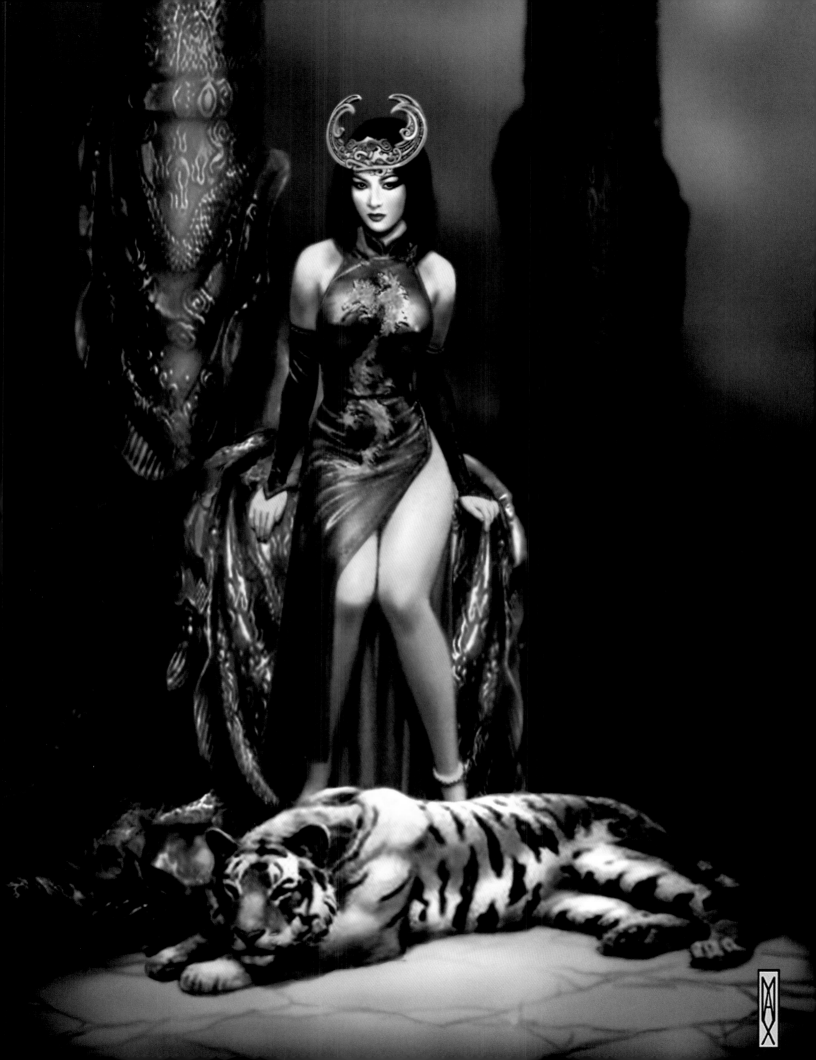

ART INDEX

AGENZIA ALFA 12

ALANNA 111

AN AWAKENING PROBLEM 110

BABYLON SLAVE 104

BATMAN 9

BEAUTY AND THE BEAST 99

BLACK PRINCESS 108

CAPTAIN AMERICA 11

CITIZEN OF THE SEA 55

CREATION 69

CYBERANGEL 113

CYBERBIKER 112

DEATH CARRIER 71

DEATH FIELD 62

DRAGON 29

DRAGON FLIGHT 56

DRAGON LADY 106

DRAGON RIDE 17

DRAGON'S NEST 70

DRAGON'S WRATH 77

ELFIC VESSEL 73

EMERALD GUARD 61

ENDORA

– Endora 84

– Lorien 85

– Elesia 86

– Endora - page 2 87

– Endora - page 3 88

– Kaltheck 89

EYMERICH 72

FAIRY FALLS 49

FIRST CONTACT 7

FLAME OF PASSION 121

FLAMING ELF 47

FREEDOM 107

FROZEN PLANET 36

GOING BACK HOME 81

GOLIATH 68

HAUNTED HOUSE 83

HORSE OF MARLY 31

KILLER HUNTERS 76

KILLING FOG 79

LADY AND DRAGON 101

LAND OF GIANTS 80

LAST ROMAN CONQUER 24

LEDA 105

LOVE TIES 124

LUTHIEN 103

MAIDEN OF THE WOODS 48

MAY 102

MAY FRAIN 75

MEGARA 65

MOUNTAIN ORCS 63

NATHAN NEVER 11, 12, 13, 14, 15

NEVERENDING YEARS - first attempt . .59

NEVERENDING YEARS - final 66

NEW BEGINNING 95

OLYMPIC POLITICS 91

ON THE LAKE 32

ONE THOUSAND HEARTS 122

PENCIL DRAWING 1 46

PENCIL DRAWING 2 51

PORTRAIT OF ROBERTA 45

RED GUARDIAN 96

RETURN OF THE ICE CRUSADERS
– Frozen Planet .36
– Crusaders already landed 38
– Explorers – pencil sketch I 39
– Explorers – pencil sketch II 39
– Explorers 39
– Crusaders on flying bikes 40
– Flying Bikes – pencil sketch 41
– Fight – pencil sketch 42
– Fight 42
– The Conclusion 43
– Woman exploring 44
SARA 25
SATYR 28
SEDUCTION 114
SERINDE 119
SHE DWELLS AMONG THE CLOUDS . .20
SILVER SURFER 27
SKY HOUNDS 58
SMILODON 29
SPACE MARINE 115
STAR BLADE 92
STAR CITY 93
STAR CORE 18
STORM 23
SUNSET ON SHADIR 50
SUPERMAN 10
SWEET WILD WIND 123
TECHNICAL CHRIME 30
TESMETH .94
THE ADVISER 52
THE BRIDE MAKER 120

THE CONQUER OF THE THRONE 97
THE EVIL INSIDE 118
THE EXPLORERS 22
THE FINAL FIGHT 57
THE GOD IN THE SKY 19
THE LADY AND THE WARRIOR 98
THE MACKENZIES – ZACK 109
THE OUTLAW AND THE LADY 34
THE PERSUADERS 116
THE RAPTURE 35
THE SORCERESS CASTLE 74
THE TIGER WARRIORS 21
THOUSAND YEARS EMPRESS 125
TROLL 26
VIOLENT BIG CITY 78
WHITE PRINCESS 53
WILDERNESS 117
WONDER WOMAN – pencil sketch 8
WONDER WOMAN 8
YELLOW SUBMARINE 67
YOUNG GALADRIEL 60

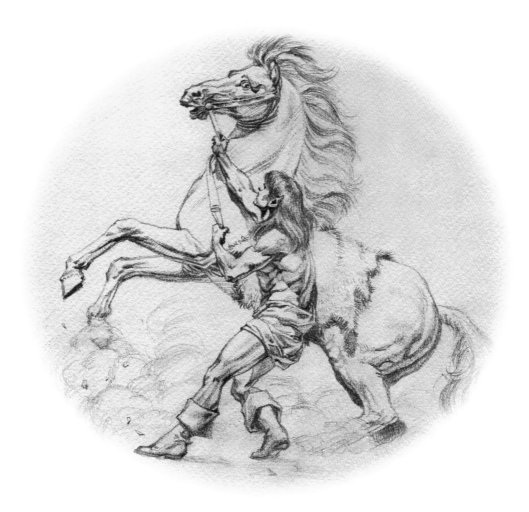

ACKNOWLEDGMENTS

Thanks to all the people who supported me through all these years, always believing in
my talent, Roberta, Ale, Stefano, Tino, my parents.
Thanks also to Paolo Peruzzo, who encouraged me when I was young, and to Antonio Serra,
who gave me a chance.
A special thanks goes to Chris Stone and Nicola Hodgson for their kindness and assistance.
I hope they enjoyed working with me as I did with them.

Finally my gratitude goes to all those who marked the pathway before me, standing on the
shoulders of these giants I could see further: William Turner, Johannes Vermeer, Edgar Degas,
Caravaggio, Giovanni Segantini, Silvestro Lega, John Singer Sargent, Edward Hopper,
Norman Rockwell, John Buscema, Neal Adams, Boris Vallejo, Frank Frazetta and
Jean-Auguste-Dominique Ingres.